The Alaska Geographic Society

To teach many more to better know and use our natural resources

Chief Editor: Robert A. Henning
Editor: Penny Rennick
Associate Editor: Kathy Doogan
Supervising Editor this issue: Liz Bryan
Designer: Pam S. Ernst

ALASKA GEOGRAPHIC®, ISSN 0361-1353, is published quarterly by The Alaska Geographic Society, Anchorage, Alaska 99509-3370. Second-class postage paid in Edmonds, Washington 98020-3588. Printed in U.S.A. Copyright© 1985 by The Alaska Geographic Society. All rights reserved. Registered trademark; Alaska Geographic, ISSN 0361-1353; Key title Alaska Geographic.

THE ALASKA GEOGRAPHIC SOCIETY is a nonprofit organization exploring new frontiers of knowledge across the lands of the polar rim, learning how other men and other countries live in their Norths, putting the geography book back in the classroom, exploring new methods of teaching and learning — sharing in the excitement of discovery in man's wonderful new world north of 51°16′.

MEMBERS OF THE SOCIETY RECEIVE *Alaska Geographic®*, a quality magazine which devotes each quarterly issue to monographic in-depth coverage of a northern geographic region or resource-oriented subject.

MEMBERSHIP DUES in The Alaska Geographic Society are $30 per year; $34 to non-U.S. addresses. (Eighty percent of each year's dues is for a one-year subscription to *Alaska Geographic®*.) Order from The Alaska Geographic Society, Box 93370, Anchorage, Alaska 99509-3370; (907) 563-1141.

MATERIAL SOUGHT: The editors of *Alaska Geographic®* seek a wide variety of informative material on the lands north of 51°16′ on geographic subjects — anything to do with resources and their uses (with heavy emphasis on quality color photography) — from Alaska, northern Canada, Siberia, Japan — all geographic areas that have a relationship to Alaska in a physical or economic sense. We do not want material done in excessive scientific terminology. A query to the editors is suggested. Payments are made for all material upon publication.

CHANGE OF ADDRESS: The post office does not automatically forward *Alaska Geographic®* when you move. To ensure continous service, notify us six weeks before moving. Send us your new address and zip code (and moving date), your old address and zip code, and if possible send a mailing label from a copy of *Alaska Geographic®*. Send this information to *Alaska Geographic®* Mailing Offices, 130 Second Avenue South, Edmonds, Washington 98020-3588.

MAILING LISTS: We have begun making our members' names and addresses available to carefully screened publications and companies whose products and activities might be of interest to you. If you would prefer not to receive such mailings, please so advise us, and include your mailing label (or your name and address if label is not available).

The Library of Congress has cataloged this serial publication as follows:

Alaska Geographic. v.1-
[Anchorage, Alaska Geographic Society] 1972-
v. ill. (part col.). 23 x 31 cm.
Quarterly.
Official publication of the Alaska Geographic Society.
Key title: Alaska geographic, ISSN 0361-1353.

1. Alaska — Description and travel — 1959-
—Periodicals.   I. Alaska Geographic Society.

F901.A266   917.98′04′505   72-92087
                                    MARC-S

Library of Congress   75[7912]

Previous page — *Sunset, west coast Vancouver Island* (Bob Herger — Photo/Graphics)
Right — *Deep forest, tall trees* (Bob Herger — Photo/Graphics)

Table of Contents

From the President

We hope to bring Alaska Geographic Society members still another "Inside Passage" edition to follow this fine British Columbia Coast issue covering the Canadian and southern end of the "Inside Passage." This upcoming edition will be "Southeast Alaska/South," proceeding north from where this B.C. Coast edition meets the southern Alaska border and ending in the Sumner Straits area where our earlier and so popular "Southeast Alaska" edition takes over the northern end of the several hundred mile long "Inside Passage."

The issue to come will cover Prince of Wales Island and the Ketchikan area in detail . . . Metlakatla, Revillagigedo, Behm Canal, Misty Fiords . . . and much more.

Meanwhile, enjoy the waters of our Canadian neighbors. They have long deep fjords, isolated fishing and logging communities, great granite buttresses of rock and redolent forests of fir and cedar, winding twisting channels everywhere that make this region a cruising tourists' delight. It is easy to see why the early Haida and other Indians loved this land, and why it is today a mecca for cruising yachtsmen as well as tourists aboard the big cruise liners.

Liz Bryan, our supervising editor of this piece, has done a fine job. But then Liz, a Vancouver resident who was an editor on our old Western Homes & Living and eventually bought that magazine with her husband and sold it as a successful Western Living, has always turned out sharp editorial work. The British Columbia government a few years ago commissioned Mrs. Bryan to write the Province's book on B.C. to end all books on B.C. . . . *British Columbia: This Favoured Land,* $16.95, Douglas & McIntyre, 1615 Venables St., Vancouver, BC V5L 2H1. Liz is a transplanted English girl, but there's a lot of love for wonderful B.C. in this one you are about to read. Enjoy. You are getting the authoritative best.

Sincerely,

Robert A. Henning

Aerial view of Vancouver, showing the inner harbor, the forested peninsula of Stanley Park and Canada Place, the new cruise ship/hotel complex built for Expo 86 (Jurgen Vogt — Photo/Graphics)

Introduction

The British Columbia Coast measures less than 500 miles from the southern tip of Vancouver Island north to Portland Canal, its boundary with Alaska. But the coastline is fragmented, torn into myriad islands and cracked by many deep and meandering fjords so the actual shoreline miles stretch to 17,000 with a staggering inventory of inlets and islets, peninsulas, coves and promontories. Onshore the topography is equally difficult, a fractured chain of high mountains standing up to their knees in the sea and covered by quilts of thick forest. It is far too complicated a labyrinth ever to be known in a single lifetime.

For untold centuries native Indians in small shoreline villages lived well off the sea and the land, leaving undisturbed the fragile equilibrium between resource use and abuse. Europeans came late. They have disfigured but never tamed this sternly vertical land that rises so steeply out of the sea. More than 75 percent of the province lies above 3,000 feet, and at this elevation there is no level and friendly plateau, but rather the land rises higher still in a spiky succession of frostbitten peaks, some still smothered in Pleistocene ice. Only along the narrow coastal margins and the few large river valleys has modern man, like the

The twin peaks called The Lions rear their snowy heads above Vancouver. (Herger-Burridge — Photo/Graphics)

Top left — *Totem, Stanley Park* (Vancouver Visitors Bureau)
Top right — *The north shore of Vancouver's False Creek, formerly an industrial area, was transformed for Expo 86. In the background, The Lions mountains.* (Gunter Marx — Photo/Graphics)
Above — *Young Nishga girls in ceremonial regalia.* (Vickie Jensen)

Indians, found a foothold, though his machines are reaching ever farther into the mountain forests.

More than 70 percent of British Columbia's population of nearly three million is concentrated in the southern lowlands. Of the rest, most live in the valleys on the eastern side of the Coast Mountains, leaving only a sprinkling of people, less than seven percent of the total, in the huge area of coastal British Columbia north of about Campbell River. The largest settlements here are Prince Rupert near the mouth of the Skeena River, with a population of about 17,000, and neighboring Kitimat at the inland end of Douglas Channel, population 12,000. The remainder are tiny, isolated communities, most of them reached only from the sea or by air.

Roads are few. The sole highway north up the coast from the lower mainland ends after ninety miles, and even this would not be possible without two ferry links across inlets. Land access from the east is hampered by the mountains that enclose the coast from the rest of Canada. Only three roads have breached this barrier: Highway 16 to Prince Rupert, Highway 20 to Bella Coola and, in the south, Highway 1, the Trans-Canada Highway, along the great valley of the Fraser. Apart from these blacktop strands of civilization and a shifting network of logging roads, the B.C.

Coast north of the Strait of Georgia is pretty well a country trackless and uninhabited.

This fact gives the British Columbia identity its particular tension, its feeling of being perched on the edge — not just of a continent but of wilderness itself. For most of the millions who live in the cosy urban environments of the south coast know and care little about the wild land to the north, the seaward side of their own province, even though they may owe their livelihoods to its resources. Some of this indifference is due to difficulty of access, for the coast is not an easy land — except to look at, misty islands and mountains wreathed in summer fog. It is too much at the mercy of the sea and the wind and the lashing rainstorms. It is also too big, too steep, too lonely; for those accustomed to an urban hum its silence brings disquiet.

But this indifference is damaging. The wilderness coast, one of the last unspoiled areas on Earth, has suffered a century of gradual degradation. Its magnificent rain forests are fast disappearing; its streams and beaches are being polluted, the future of its fish and wildlife seems uncertain. City people in general seem not to care. But those who venture by small boat among the inlets and islands, or who hike in to its mountain solitudes, are aware of the changes. The land is still beautiful, but they worry about its future.

Formation

In terms of physical geography, the British Columbia Coast is divided longitudinally into three: two high ranges of mountains separated by a depression known as the Coastal Trough. This trough stretches north from Puget Sound to Dixon Entrance and varies in width from one hundred miles at the Fraser Delta to a ten-mile neck called the Seymour Arch, near Kelsey Bay in Johnstone Strait. It is mostly submerged by the Pacific Ocean: only small licks of land along the mainland coast and the islands can properly be called lowland. All the rest can be measured in terms of the vertical, the Insular Mountains accounting for nearly all of Vancouver Island and the Queen Charlottes, the Coast Range forming a prickly barrier one hundred miles wide along the mainland's western edge.

These mountains are complex, composed of folded and faulted sedimentary and volcanic rocks (the remains of very ancient islands and sea basins) pushed up in several stages over millions of years by large underlying masses of molten magma. This magma, known as the coast batholith, slowly rose like giant blisters, cooling and crystallizing into a coarse-grained aggregate of granite. Constant stream erosion over later millenia ultimately stripped away the softer coverings

Left — *Climbers camped on the Tiedemann Glacier are overshadowed by the tumbling ice of Munday Glacier which spills down the flanks of Mount Waddington in the Coast Range.* (Jack Bryan)
Right — *From an altitude of 35,000 feet, huge glaciers near Mount Waddington look like giant ribbons or highways of ice.* (J. Burridge — Photo/Graphics)

Above — *Their valleys deepened by glacial scouring, the mountains along the ocean edges were drowned as the sea levels rose to form a maze of islands and inlets.* (J. Burridge — Photo/Graphics)

Left — *The Mainland coast is a sea of granite mountains, their peaks sharpened by millenia of ice.* (J. Burridge — Photo/Graphics)

Right — *The Monarch Icefield in the Coast Mountains southeast of Bella Coola presents a view of the land as it must have been during the Pleistocene Era, smothered with a thick blanket of ice and snow.* (J. Burridge — Photo/Graphics)

of sedimentary rock. The underlying granite, though very hard, was not impervious to erosion; rain and frost and time ground slowly but inexorably away to shape its surface. Eons later there began a second volcanic thrust, which pushed up the batholiths and the remnant traces of older materials into the high Coast Mountains.

Mountain building (the technical term is orogeny) along the western coast of North America is attributed to movement of the earth's crust along fault lines which divide the globe's surface into several large jigsaw-puzzle tectonic plates. As these crustal plates slide over one another, the underneath plates melt, the top ones are buckled and pushed up to form mountains. The North American plate, it is believed, continues to inch westward over the Pacific Ocean plate, and the mountains may still be growing. Scientists are not sure of this because of another phenomenon that began in the Pleistocene Era, about two million years ago: the last Ice Age.

For reasons not yet known, temperatures around the world

suddenly drop. Ice forms at the poles and in the mountains, and gradually spreads out over the land. Scientists know this has happened several times in Earth's history, and some attribute it to a shift in Earth's solar orbit. At the height of the most recent Ice Age, most of Canada was covered by a frozen blanket several thousand feet thick that inched down from the eastern Arctic. Except for the northeastern corner, British Columbia was not touched by this continental ice but its mountains produced an ice sheet of their own, known as the Cordilleran. At first the ice cover was scant, merely small alpine glaciers stretching into tongues of ice which moved down into the mountain valleys. As these glaciers grew they merged into huge icefields which gradually covered most of the province. From the divide of the mainland Coast Range, ice flowed generally east onto the Interior Plateau and west down the steep slopes into the sea. On the mountains of the islands, less ice built up because of the warming effect of the surrounding ocean, but it, too, flowed down the valleys into the sea. All of British Columbia, except for the very highest peaks and a few possible refuges on the Queen Charlottes and Vancouver Island, was blanketed by ice, not once but at least three times as temperatures fluctuated. It was ice that gave the land of British Columbia its present contours.

As glaciers move they pick up and carry with them huge quantities of rock and earth. These materials scrape and scour the bedrock over which the ice moves, deepening and steepening the valleys, smoothing out the hills. Where the glaciers reach the sea, icebergs calve and melt, dropping their attached boulders and debris onto the ocean floor.

The most recent ice sheet (the only one that has left clear traces) began its retreat about 10,000 years ago. As it melted it dropped the earth and rock it was carrying, leaving a thick

Left — *The sheer granite hump of the Stawamus Chief near Squamish is a challenge for rock-climbers from all over North America.* (Phil Hersee)
Previous spread — *Remnant tongue of the icefields that once covered the B.C. mountains, Wedgemount Glacier spills into a small mountain tarn in Garibaldi Provincial Park.* (Greg Maurer — Photo/Graphics)

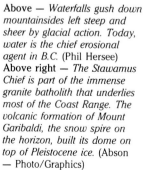

Above — *Waterfalls gush down mountainsides left steep and sheer by glacial action. Today, water is the chief erosional agent in B.C.* (Phil Hersee)
Above right — *The Stawamus Chief is part of the immense granite batholith that underlies most of the Coast Range. The volcanic formation of Mount Garibaldi, the snow spire on the horizon, built its dome on top of Pleistocene ice.* (Abson — Photo/Graphics)

layer of this glacial till spread over the land. Huge quantities of meltwater turned the smallest mountain streams into dashing rivers, rivers into rampaging floods, valleys into lakes, and the glacial debris was cut into and washed downhill onto the lowlands and into the sea.

The ice has not all gone. In the mainland ranges huge icefields remain, particularly among the towering mountain massifs between latitudes 50 and 52, and nearly every mountain of any size still carries alpine glaciers, some of them enormous ice roads. Even where the ice has long gone, the land bears its unmistakable imprint. Mountains engulfed by the ice sheet were scraped round and smooth. Nunataks (peaks that protruded above the ice like rocky islands) were etched by alpine glaciers into sharp horn shapes with thin,

serrated ridges, cols and basins. Everywhere are hanging valleys and waterfalls, and the deeply scoured, U-shaped larger valleys are sometimes still humped by moraines of glacial debris.

The magnificent fjords of the coast are part of the Ice Age legacy. They are steep river valleys, deepened by ice action and subsequently flooded by the sea. Known in B.C. mostly as inlets or channels, these fjords are narrow, from half to two miles wide, but up to sixty miles long and deeper than fifty fathoms. (Deepest is Finlayson Channel, which sounds to 418 fathoms along the east side of Swindle Island.) Their sides are steep and high, going from sea level to 6,000 and 8,000 feet, with hanging valleys and beautiful cascading waterfalls.

The Ice Age also affected the levels of the ocean and the land. Sea levels dropped because the water supply froze and the tremendous weight of the ice sheet pushed Earth's crust down, as much as a thousand feet in the Fraser Valley. When the ice melted the ocean quickly rose again, but the Earth was slower to respond. The sea rose much higher than before onto the still sunken land, deeply flooding the glacially deepened coastal lowlands and river valleys and leaving marine deposits of shells along beaches that are now high and dry on mountain shoulders. (On Vancouver's north shore the upper level, now traversed by Highway 1, was once a shoreline terrace.) Earth's crust has gradually bounced back, but scientists do not yet know whether it has reached equilibrium. Some land still appears to be rising, but this could be the continuation of a mountain-building phase.

The west coast of North America, where crustal plates collide, is a land still in upheaval. Mountain-building itself is too slow for man's limited timespan to notice, but more

Above — Aerial view of the community of Crescent Beach and the mouth of the Nicomekl River, south of Vancouver. The river is one of two small streams that drain the Fraser's floodplain. (Tony Swain)
Right — The coastline, fretted with inlets and islands, provides sheltered but intricate shipping channels. This is Hole-in-the-Wall in the Strait of Georgia. (Carolyn Angus — Photo/Graphics)

Above — *The huge and powerful Fraser River is still building its delta out into the Pacific at the rate of 28 feet a year. Delta lands are fertile. This is Mud Bay north of White Rock.* (Tony Swain)

Left — *Scenic Shannon Falls, south of Squamish, plummets steeply into the deep fjord of Howe Sound.* (Bill Staley)

violent earth spasms, earthquakes and volcanic activity, make themselves known. The great Denali fault line lies off the B.C. Coast close to the western shores of the Queen Charlotte Islands, and the whole coastline is subject to earthquakes. Several have been recorded here — the largest, which registered 8.1 on the Richter scale of 9, was in the Queen Charlottes in 1949 — so far with only minor damage because of sparse population. Small earthquakes have also taken place close to major urban areas around Georgia Strait, and the threat of large-scale damage is always present. Vancouver, mostly built on unstable glacial and alluvial deposits, is particularly vulnerable.

There are no active volcanoes along the B.C. Coast today, though there is ample evidence of past action, most impressively around Mount Garibaldi, a relatively young volcano which erupted and built its lava cone on top of the Pleistocene ice sheet. Part of the cone collapsed when the ice melted, so the mountain today does not have the "icecream cone" profile typical of volcanoes along the West Coast of the United States. A cinder cone eight hundred feet high on the southwestern edge of Swindle Island, and a higher conical hill of volcanic tuff on nearby Lake Island, in Mathieson Channel, show no signs of glaciation and are considered to be post-Pleistocene. Much more recent are the lava flows in the Nass Valley, which at one time blocked the Tseaux River, then spread out to form a plain seven miles long and three miles wide which is still almost devoid of vegetation. This lava is thought to be no older than three hundred years, and the event is commemorated in Indian tribal history.

Other evidence of seismic activity can be found in the number of hot springs along the coast, notably on the west coast of Vancouver Island, the southern Queen Charlottes, the central coast, and the Harrison-Lillooet area of the southern Fraser drainage.

Right — *Steep mountainsides bear the scars of numerous avalanche tracks. Trees grow only slowly on this rugged terrain.* (J. Burridge — Photo/Graphics)

Landforms

Island Profile

The mountains of the islands are on the whole much lower than those on the mainland. They reach a maximum on Vancouver Island of just over 7,000 feet; on the Charlottes, of less than 3,700 feet. (Peaks on the mainland commonly rise more than 9,000 feet.) Nevertheless, island mountains are steep and rugged and bear the scars of intense glaciation, in many places down to and below present sea level.

Along the 150-mile length of the Queen Charlotte archipelago, from Cape Knox in the north to Cape St. James in the south, the San Cristoval Mountains are mostly granite and rise steeply from the sea, facing the full onslaught of North Pacific storms. Here, high seas have fretted the coastline into cliffs, pinnacles, stacks and sea caves, erosion which elsewhere produces beaches of sand and gravel. Here, because the land is at the very edge of the continental shelf, the eroded sediments plunge into deep water and are swept out to sea. Only a few small coves of polished gravel and reefs of black volcanic rock relieve the severity of this sheer, deeply incised west coast, a coast which is buffeted by the highest winds in all of Canada.

The eastern sides of the mountains slope more gradually through a transitional plateau down to the Queen Charlotte

Left — *South entrance to Silva Bay in the Gulf Islands. Gabriola Island lies on the left, small Sear Island on the right.* (Tony Swain)
Right — *Sunset over Skidegate Inlet on the Queen Charlotte Islands. In the distance, the San Cristoval Mountains are still tipped with snow.* (Jurgen Vogt — Photo/Graphics)

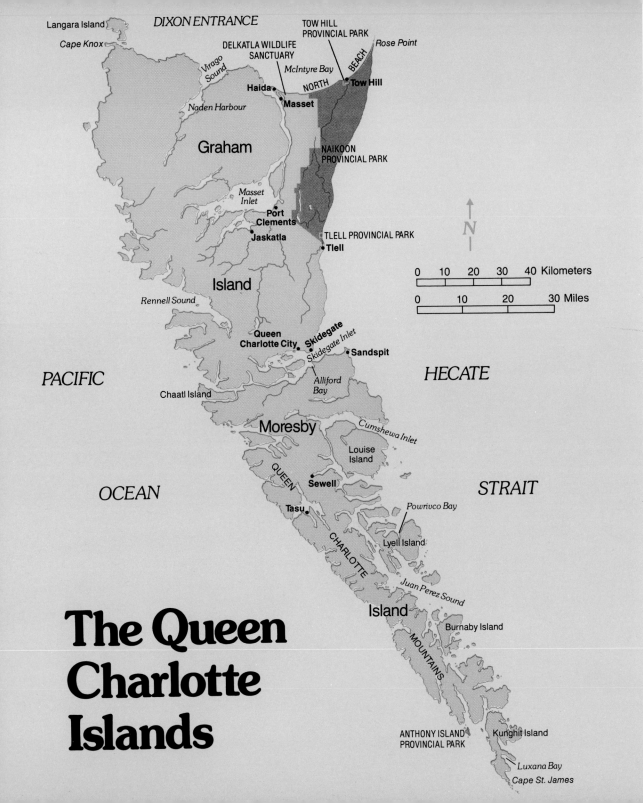

Langara Island

Cape Knox

DIXON ENTRANCE

TOW HILL
PROVINCIAL PARK

DELKATLA WILDLIFE
SANCTUARY

Rose Point

Virago
Sound

McIntyre Bay

BEACH

NORTH

Haida

Naden Harbour

Masset

Tow Hill

Graham

NAIKOON
PROVINCIAL PARK

Masset
Inlet

Port
Clements

Jaskatla

TLELL PROVINCIAL PARK

Tlell

Island

Rennell Sound

10 20 30 40 Kilometers

N

0 10 20 30 Miles

Queen
Charlotte City

Skidegate

Skidegate Inlet

Sandspit

PACIFIC

HECATE

Chaatl Island

Alliford
Bay

Moresby

Cumshewa Inlet

Louise
Island

OCEAN

QUEEN

Sewell

STRAIT

Tasu

Powrivco Bay

Lyell Island

The Queen Charlotte Islands

Island

Burnaby Island

CHARLOTTE

MOUNTAINS

ANTHONY ISLAND
PROVINCIAL PARK

Kunghit Island

Luxana Bay

Cape St. James

Top — *The long scimitar of Rose Spit is a sandbar swept up by wind and sea currents at the northeastern tip of Graham Island in the Queen Charlottes.* (B.C. Government)
Above — *Two Haida Indians dig for clams on the sandy sweep of Rose Spit.* (Jurgen Vogt — Photo/Graphics)
Right — *Cape St. James, at the southern end of the Queen Charlotte archipelago, was named by Captain George Dixon when he sailed by on St. James Day in 1787. On the cape is a meteorological station and 44-foot lighthouse tower.* (David Hatler)

lowlands which occupy the northeast corner of Graham, the largest and most northerly of the more than 150 islands. These lowlands are composed of basaltic lava, sedimentary rocks and glacial till, and slope down to the broad Argonaut Plain, the result of massive sedimentary and post-glacial outwash. Where this plain slopes into the sea there is a remarkable sand and gravel beach, seventy-five miles long and several hundred yards wide along the east and northern shores of Graham Island. This magnificent, lonely beach, backed by huge banks of bleached driftwood and a forest of salt-stunted trees, is broken only by the abrupt cliffs of Tow Hill, a 500-foot-high volcanic remnant. At the extreme northeastern tip of the island is Rose Spit, a thin, trailing sandbar formed by beach gravels swept constantly northward by winds and sea currents. This whole wild northeast coast of Graham Island has been set aside as a B.C. provincial park called Naikoon, the Haida Indian word for nose. A park trail beside the Yakoun River leads to the famous Golden Spruce, a forest freak some sixty feet high with beautiful bright yellow needles, a flame in the dark surrounding forest.

The Queen Charlottes are rugged, steep and so intricately fractured by the sea that agriculture, settlement and road-building are limited mostly to the lowlands of Graham Island and north Moresby, the second largest island. The sea and the air provide primary transportation to the rest of the island communities.

Vancouver Island, higher in elevation than the Charlottes, was less drowned by the returning post-glacial seas and thus has remained a single landmass, though deeply fingered by the ocean along the steep west coast. One fjord, Alberni Inlet, almost cuts the island in two at its midpoint and another, Quatsino Sound, almost severs its northwestern tip. The

Above right — The Queen Charlottes are among the wettest places on earth. Heavy rainfall year-round produces huge, dank rain forests deeply quilted with moss. (Bob Herger — Photo/Graphics)
Right — The beaches on the west coast of Vancouver Island, where the shallow continental shelf permits sedimentary deposition, are wide and sandy, backed by fences of bleached driftwood hurled ashore by Pacific storms. (Lyn Hancock)

Top left — *In good weather, lace-edged waves wash rhythmically ashore onto the broad, sandy scallop of Long Beach on the west coast of Vancouver Island. The beach is within Pacific Rim National Park.* (Council of Forest Industries)

Above — *A storm sweeps in at Amphitrite Point near Ucluelet, west coast of Vancouver Island.* (Lyn Hancock)

Top right — *Aerial view looking east over Montague Harbor, a favourite rendezvous for recreational boaters on Galiano Island.* (Tony Swain)

Right — *Tow Hill, an abrupt cliff of volcanic basalt, rises 500 feet above the miles of sandy beaches that line the northeastern edges of Graham Island in the Charlottes. Naikoon Provincial Park protects all this shoreline and the forests of low-lying Argonaut Plain which lies behind.* (B.C. Government)

highest mountains are in the middle of the island (Mount Golden Hinde, 7,219 feet, is just about on the geographical centre). These mountains are a mixture of softer sedimentary and volcanic rock with granite intrusions, and though they rise steeply from the sea along the western shore, eroded sediments have settled in the shallower seas of the continental shelf to form a slim coastal plain that fringes the southern two-thirds of the west coast. Action by wind and waves upon the sedimentary rocks and glacial materials of the shore has created here some spectacular beaches. Best known are Wickaninnish and Long Beach, huge arcs of sand between the fishing ports of Tofino and Ucluelet, now part of Pacific Rim National Park, and there are many others: Escalante, Bamfield, Pachena, Clo-ose, Sombrio and China Beach, Jordan River and Point No Point, each one of sand or pebbles or rock enclosed by mothering arms of harder rock. In places, deposits of sandstone or shale have been worn by the waves into rocky ledges and chiselled into tidepools.

Like the Charlottes, the east side of Vancouver Island's mountains slope more gradually toward the sheltered waters of Georgia Strait, which narrowly separates the island from the mainland. The waters of the strait are shallow and protected from offshore weather. Sediments washed eastward from the mountains have built up a generous coastal plain and gently sloping sand beaches, up to a mile wide at low tide at places such as Parksville and Qualicum. The sheltered lowlands of south and east Vancouver Island provide a gentle landscape conducive to agriculture and settlement, unlike the lowlands of the extreme northern tip, which are buffeted by winds from north and west. A network of roads runs around the shore from Port Renfrew in the southwest to Port Hardy in the northeast, but few penetrate the mountain barrier to reach the rugged west coast.

Within the sheltered waters of Georgia Strait are the Gulf Islands, the Canadian part of Washington State's San Juan Islands. These are mostly the rocky outcrops of a drowned landscape, smothered and smoothed by glacial ice, though some, such as Savary and Hernando, are hummocks of sand and gravel left when the glaciers receded.

Above — *Coastal alluvial plain near Maple Bay, east coast Vancouver Island; Gulf Islands in the background.* (Lyn Hancock)
Right — *While the beaches of Vancouver Island's protected east coast are mostly of pebble, they shelve very gently and large numbers of holiday-makers come to swim here in the warm and shallow waters of Georgia Strait.* (Marin Petkov — Photo/Graphics)

Gulls whiten the sand flats of a small beach along the West Coast Trail on Vancouver Island. (David Hatler)

The Mainland Coast

The Coast Mountains of the mainland are high, rugged and continuous. The western ranges are almost entirely of resistant granite and quartz diorite, their softer sedimentary coverings long since worn and washed away. The highest peaks lie in the Pacific Ranges south of the Bella Coola River, where many reach more than 10,000 feet and the highest, Mount Waddington, to 13,177 feet. (Waddington is the second highest mountain in B.C.; only Mount Fairweather on the B.C.-Alaska border is higher, 15,300 feet.) Covered by the Pleistocene ice cap up to 8,000 feet above sea level, the Coast Mountains bear the firm imprint of tremendous ice coverage and erosion. Huge icefields and glaciers yet remain, particularly around Mounts Waddington and Silverthrone and between the Homathco and Southgate Rivers where the landscape seems still locked in the last Ice Age.

Only a few great rivers have cut through these mountains from the east, but they are deeply penetrated from the west by many long fjords, making it possible to go by boat right into the mountain heartland. The thin strip of lowland and maze of offshore islands lie below two-thousand feet but the topography here is also rough and rugged from glaciation. Everywhere, exposed bedrock shows the scars. Except for the river valleys, the mainland coast is too steep and rocky for serious agriculture or settlement, too dissected by the sea for roads. But sheltered for the most part by the two large offshore island groups, Vancouver Island and the Charlottes, its waters provide one of the best marine highways in the

Right — Fluted ice spires and mountain mists create an ethereal backdrop for a climber on Mount Waddington. (Jack Bryan) Opposite page — Mount Waddington, B.C.'s second highest peak, is a long, tough ascent for mountain climbers. The Plummer hut, here shown under construction, was built on a nearby saddle. Its roof trusses and lumber were dropped by helicopter. (Jack Bryan)

The Royal Hudson is a steam train that runs up Howe Sound between North Vancouver and Squamish in the summer months. Passengers enjoy superb mountain scenery. (Vancouver Visitors Bureau)
Right — Below the perpetual snows of the Coast Mountain summits, alpine meadows in summer are ablaze with scarlet paintbrush, lupin and valerian. (Fred Chapman — Photo/Graphics)

A study in pink and purple: looking west over Howe Sound and the lights of the town of Squamish at the inlet head. (Fred Chapman — Photo/Graphics)

world, a protected and scenic route for both commercial and recreational shipping. The Inside Passage to Alaska is today a well-known tourist attraction, providing for most cruise passengers the only glimpse they will ever have of the mountainous shores.

Rivers

The great mountains of the British Columbia Coast are cut by equally great rivers: from north to south, the Nass, Skeena, Bella Coola, Kliniklini, Homathko and Fraser. The greatest of these by far is the Fraser; it is 850 miles long from its headwaters in the Rocky Mountains to the sea, and it drains nearly 90,000 square miles of the British Columbia heartland. In its passage through the mountains it has carved tremendous trenches and granite canyons and scoured away deep drifts of glacial debris, building up at its mouth an immense delta whose land today stretches back a hundred miles to Hope. This delta blocked the mouths of several long fjords, landlocking them into lakes (Pitt, Alouette, and Harrison lakes were all once embayments of the sea), and continues to build out into the Strait of Georgia at an average rate of twenty-eight feet a year.

The Skeena rises high in the Skeena Mountains of the interior system, east of the Coast Range, and flows 360 miles to the sea just south of the Alaska boundary near Prince Rupert. It and the other rivers which run west through the Coast Mountains are not very long, but because they drain

Left — *Chatterbox Falls at the head of Princess Louisa Inlet.*
(Lyn Hancock)
Above — *Aerial photo of Swindle Island on the northwest coast, part of the thickly forested coastal trough.* (Lyn Hancock)

The Fraser Valley is contained along its southern edge by steep mountains of the Cascade Range. The valley is the chief agricultural area of the province, specializing in dairy products and soft fruits. (Jack Bryan)

areas of very high precipitation, they are powerful and destructive agents of erosion that carry tons of sediment down to the ocean. Many of them enter the sea at the ends of long deep-water fjords, however, so this sediment seldom accumulates into a delta.

The Sea Floor

British Columbia's continental shelf, an area of shallow seas less than 450 feet deep, extends offshore for roughly 100 miles, dropping off very steeply into the deep Queen Charlotte Trough a few miles off the western edge of the Charlottes, and less steeply about 20 miles west of Vancouver Island. In places the shelf itself, exposed to the air when sea levels dropped, has been scoured by Ice Age glaciers.

Beyond the continental shelf, the deep sea floor which plunges to depths of below 10,000 feet is far from flat. Like the land to the east, it is scarred by trenches, scooped out into basins and canyons, and humped up into ridges. Most remarkable are the clusters of submarine mountains called seamounts, which rise steeply from the great depths of the Abyssal Plain often to within one hundred feet of the sea surface. On land, these 10,000-foot peaks would rival all but the very highest of the Coast Range. Mostly conical in shape, they were most likely formed by molten magma squeezing up through rifts in the Earth's crust, literally drowned volcanoes. On their slopes live varieties of marine life not found elsewhere in B.C. waters, in particular several varieties of white and black corals.

Above — The frosted peaks of Golden Ears Mountain rise to the north above the green meadows of the Fraser Valley near Langley. (Jack Bryan)

Right — Alluvial outwash from the Fraser River has built up a huge and fertile valley which stretches a hundred miles from Hope to Vancouver. At one time the mountains here had their feet in the sea, not in meadows. (Phil Hersee)

Climate

While earth forces and glaciation shaped the landforms of the British Columbia Coast, the effects of climate continue to alter the look of the landscape. On the whole, the Pacific shores enjoy the mildest and wettest climate in Canada, in fact, one of the wettest in the world. In simple terms, the higher western slopes of the mountains receive the most precipitation, while eastern slopes and lowlands in the lee of the mountains receive substantially less. This statement does nothing to describe the dramatic swing of variables. Average rainfall at Estevan Point, on the west coast of Vancouver Island, tops 120 inches a year; on the high western slopes of the mountains, as much as 240 inches, while at Victoria, not many miles to the south, only 26 inches. Vancouver airport in the Fraser delta receives 40 inches, while 15 miles north and 2,000 feet higher, the shoulders of Mount Seymour average 130 inches.

The chief factors controlling the coastal weather pattern are the ocean, the prevailing westerly winds, and the topography of the land. The Pacific is the largest of the world's oceans and relatively warm. Pushed onto the shores by the Kuroshio, or Japanese Current, its surface temperature around 60 degrees F. in summer, 40 degrees F. in winter,

Left — B.C.'s climate changes dramatically with the topography. The popular ski slopes of Mount Seymour directly overlook the city of Vancouver, where roses bloom in November and spring flowers in February. (Jack Bryan)

it is itself an enormously moderating influence, keeping summers cool and winters warm. January temperatures in southern Vancouver Island are generally in the 40s, a good 20 degrees warmer than normal for the latitude, while July averages are between 60 and 65 degrees F., only a little warmer than Aklavik in the Arctic. The growing season is the longest in Canada, with most of the coast enjoying more than 180 frost-free days a year. In balmy Victoria, this number jumps to more than 280.

Because of the stabilizing influence of the ocean, temperatures along the coast differ more with elevation than with latitude, falling only a few degrees from south to north but plunging steeply as the land rises. This makes possible one of Vancouver's special attractions: skiing on the North Shore mountains while the city parks below are bright with cherry blossom and spring flowers.

Blowing onto the coast across thousands of miles of warm seas, the prevailing westerly winds become moisture-saturated. When they run into the mountains they are forced up into cooler altitudes and the moisture condenses as rain or snow. Thus the first mountains in the winds' path, those of Vancouver Island, the Queen Charlottes and the unprotected strip of central coast, receive the most rain. As the air drops over the eastern slopes, it warms and retains its moisture, only to spill it again when it bumps into the higher peaks of the mainland ranges. The warm, wet winds are also responsible for the great banks of fog which often lie offshore and blanket the outer coastal regions.

The indented nature of the coastline produces certain inconsistencies. For instance, rainfall is often extremely heavy at the heads of some of the inlets many miles inland. The long, narrow fjords funnel and compress the oncoming

Above left — *Colorful umbrellas brighten Vancouver's winter streets. The B.C. Coast endures the wettest, though mildest, climate in Canada.* (Jurgen Vogt — Photo/Graphics)
Left — *Rainbows are common in this land of so much rain. This one soars over Vargas Island, west coast Vancouver Island.* (David Hatler)

air mass, and when it rises against the high spine of the Coast Mountains, the resultant rainfall at the inlet head is many times greater than at the mouth, though both are at sea level. In summer, temperatures at inlet heads — even those far to the north — are often a good ten degrees higher than the local average. Not only does air tend to pond in these areas and warm up, but occasionally hotter continental air pushes through the mountains from the east.

In the rain shadow of Vancouver Island, the tiny Gulf Islands enjoy a semi-desert existence, with rainfall less than twenty-five inches and cactus in bloom — within view of mountain glaciers on the mainland.

Winters at and near sea level along the southern coast are generally rainy and overcast, gloomy but mild, with snow only a rare and fleeting experience. Less than fifteen percent of the total precipitation in the south falls as snow (and most of this at higher elevations only), but this increases to around fifty percent along the north coast. Prince Rupert's winters, though only a few degrees colder than Vancouver's, are regularly snowbound.

Coastal summers tend to be mild and rainy, too. But sometimes the westerly winds are overridden by stronger forces from the Arctic or the continental interior. These can bring winter deep-freeze conditions, as they did in November of 1985, or a hot, dry summer spell, both startling exceptions to the regular temperature pattern.

Land Cover

West Coast scenery is synonymous with trees. Great forests of red cedar and hemlock, Douglas fir and Sitka spruce have taken possession of this mountainous maritime land, this enormous maze of channels and fjords and more than 7,000 islands. Were they here before the ice sheet scoured the bedrock clean of living things? Did their seeds survive, somehow, the cataclysms of ice and flood? Or did they creep slowly in from the south after the long Ice Age winter?

Scientists now believe that some parts of the Queen Charlotte Islands and the extreme westerly tip of Vancouver Island were not totally engulfed by ice, and that here dwarf versions of the sturdy lodgepole pine and mountain hemlock managed to endure the intense cold, and thus give the regenerating post-glacial forests of the coast a head start. Studies of fossilized pollens certainly show that forests have been here for a very long time — about 14,000 years — and have overcome natural catastrophes such as fire, flood, drought and even the cold. For here conditions for growth seem to be ideal: the soil is podzolic (leached of surface minerals) and well drained, the rainfall is high, the winters short and mild, the long growing season relatively sunny and bright.

Left — *B.C.'s mainland and islands are cloaked in dense evergreen forests which grow tall in the wet, mild climate.* (Bob Herger — Photo/Graphics) Right — *Some of the trees are giants. This is believed to be Canada's largest, an enormous Dougas fir growing in the Nimpkish Valley near Port Renfrew, Vancouver Island.* (Bob Herger — Photo/Graphics)

Coniferous forests mantle all the valleys and all but the highest peaks of B.C.'s mountainous terrain. In this Vancouver Island valley, a trail of lighter green deciduous trees lines the water course. (Council of Forest Industries)

Right — *Red bracket fungus brings a spot of sharp color to the dim rain forest, one of many different kinds that thrive in B.C. woodlands.* (David Hatler)

Right — *Old man's beard lichen or Spanish moss hangs from the branches, a sure sign of very damp climate and clean air.* (Richard Wright — Photo/Graphics)
Far right — *Young Douglas firs, their branches smothered in moss, grow in the shade of tall Western red cedars, an illustration of the natural forest succession.* (Bob Herger — Photo/Graphics)

Seen from the air, B.C.'s forest cover seems uniform, but in reality the forest changes in makeup because each tree species has slightly different preferences and tolerances. Douglas fir, for example, likes drier locations; western red cedar, richer soil; hemlock, more moisture; Sitka spruce is tolerant of salt spray. Other species, such as mountain hemlock and yellow cedar, prefer higher slopes. Generally, though, most of the forest at low and middle elevations along the coast can be classified as Coastal Western Hemlock. This is the classic rain forest, in the lumberman's eyes the most productive area in Canada.

Within this rain forest there are two kinds of climax tree cover: a cedar-hemlock combination and Douglas fir. While each has its preferences for optimum growth, they will replace each other in the natural sequence of forest succession. For cedar and hemlock seedlings thrive in deep shade, while young Douglas firs will grow only in the light, on slopes opened to the sun and the sky by fire or logging. The cedar-hemlock dynasty, left undisturbed, endures for centuries, each new generation of trees growing in the dark shade of its parents. But when fire or some other disaster levels the forest, it is the seeds of the Douglas fir, Canada's tallest tree, which spring quickly and vigorously to life, crowding out any others. Douglas fir forests will thrive for five hundred years, mostly on drier, southern slopes. But growing quietly in their shade are seedlings of cedar and hemlock, waiting for the newcomers to topple and rot so they can regain ascendency.

Cedar-hemlock forests thrive in wet lowlands, deluged by rain. Western hemlock, once marketed as Alaska pine, is more numerous than its associate, western red cedar, the tree that supplied the native Indians with much of their material needs. In wetter areas still, amabilis fir and yellow cedar can be found. The growth of another rain forest giant, the Sitka spruce, is determined less by forest succession than by altitude (never above a thousand feet) and proximity to the sea (never more than fifty miles distant). The most salt-tolerant (and least shade-resistant) of the conifers, it is often the only tree growing along the western coastal strip, particularly in the Queen Charlotte Islands. Prized for its high

Top — *Forest near Skidegate Mission on the Charlottes.* (Jurgen Vogt — Photo/Graphics)
Above — *The flowers of the dogwood tree are B.C.'s official emblem.* (Bill Staley)
Right — *A young dogwood in full bloom lights up the margins of a Douglas fir forest.* (Bob Herger — Photo/Graphics)
Opposite page — *Cathedral Grove, a small remnant of virgin Douglas fir forest, is a wayside park on Vancouver Island. The trees stand 275 feet tall.* (Bob Herger — Photo/Graphics)

Above — *Foxgloves bloom in great clumps along the edges of second-growth forest.* (Jack Bryan)
Left — *Above the treeline the land is frozen and snow-covered for most of the year, but during the brief summer its meadows burst into brilliant bloom. This is Harmony Bowl in Garibaldi Provincial Park.* (Vlado Matisic — Photo/Graphics)

The delicate miniature bells of twinflower carpet the mossy floors of the springtime forest. (B.C. Government)

Skunk cabbage (top) and swamp laurel or kalmia (above) bloom in the dampest parts of the forest. (Jack Bryan)

strength-to-weight ratio, Sitka spruce was used to make airplanes during the first and second world wars and today, for guitars and violins. Here, too, is the lodgepole pine that survived the Ice Age, though this tree that grows so slim and straight in the forests of the B.C. interior appears on the coast in so different a form, stunted and contorted, that it is given a different common name, shore pine.

Two hundred years of logging have all but wiped out the climax or virgin rain forests of the coast, for they were easily accessible from the shore, easy for pioneer loggers to reach and transport. Today only a few small stands, such as Cathedral Grove on Vancouver Island, remain. Reached by the highway which runs across Vancouver Island to the beaches of the west coast, Cathedral Grove is thirty acres of original forest within a larger provincial park, given to the people of B.C. by forestry magnate H.R. MacMillan in 1944. Here, ancient Douglas firs tower 250 feet high, the thickest more than ten feet in diameter. But this forest remnant is doomed. The trees are infected with a type of fungus which eats the wood from inside; they are becoming hollow shells and could fall at any time.

Just north, however, lies another relict section of unlogged forest which has been proposed as a provincial ecological reserve, a 39-acre island in the Nimpkish River. Here, where

Left — *A sinuous arbutus tree in the Gulf Islands has shed nearly all its bark. Thriving only in the dry forest zone, the arbutus is a relative of the madrona which grows down the coast south to Mexico.* (Bob Herger — Photo/Graphics)

Above — *An evergreen hardwood, the arbutus has glossy, broad leaves and coppery-red bark which is shed yearly. Its flowers are creamy, its berries crimson.* (Lyn Hancock)

soil and climate conditions are optimal, western red cedars and hemlocks grow more than 200 feet tall and there are at least 50 huge Douglas firs, not past their prime like those in Cathedral Grove but 250 to 300 feet high and still growing. Some are approaching 400 years old; they could reach a thousand. Preserving these forest giants has a high price: timber on the tiny island has been valued at $1.5 million.

The biggest tree in Canada, (though not the tallest) is likely the Red Creek Douglas fir growing in the Nimpkish Valley near Port Renfrew. It is massive, over 40 feet in girth and 240 feet high. Overwhelmed by its size, the logging company, B.C. Forest Products, has left it standing, a towering Gulliver among the Brobdingnagians of a fallen forest.

Most of the coast forest of today is second or third growth; the trees are younger and smaller than in the mature rain forest, and more sunlight filters through to the forest floor. The undergrowth thrives: it is green gone mad — all kinds of ferns and grasses, salal and salmonberry, foam flowers, fairy bells, bunchberry, devil's club, wild lily-of-the-valley and ginger. Tree branches are wrapped with moss sponges and hung with lichens; fallen logs quilted with green play nursemaid to sprouting seedlings. Many kinds of mushrooms of different shape and color grow not only on the ground but on logs and on living trees.

Deciduous trees such as red alder, vine and big-leaf maple grow in slide areas and logged clearings, along with flowering shrubs and berries. The alder, spurned by foresters as a weed, is a most valuable forest asset, not only because it is the first tree to take over a devastated area, but because microbes growing on its roots return nitrogen to the soil. Forest bogs are bright in spring with yellow skunk cabbage; in summer, with Labrador tea and the pale, dimpled flowers of swamp laurel.

In the rain shadow of the Vancouver Island mountains, the lowlands around the Strait of Georgia receive on average only a third of the moisture of the western rain forest, and those drier conditions favor the growth of Douglas fir. Because of accessibility and demand for the straight, tall timbers of the giant firs, these forests were the first to be

Above left — *In the rain-shadow belt, particularly on the Gulf Islands, the climate is dry enough for opuntia cacti to grow and blossom.* (Liz Bryan)

Above right — *Pussy willow buds shake their pollen in the wind.* (Jack Bryan)

Above — *One of B.C.'s protected wildflowers, the pale pink trillium grows in coastal woods.* (B.C. Government)

Opposite page — *The forests of the outer coast are very wet, spongy with mosses, like this one in the Queen Charlottes.* (David Hatler)

Far left, top — *Lichen in many shades of red, green and brown illustrate the dampness of the B.C. forest.* (Jack Bryan)

Far left, bottom — *Leaves of the vine maple turn scarlet in the fall.* (Bill Staley)

51

The Chilliwack River, a tributary of the Fraser, runs through dense second-growth forest where branches and river boulders alike are verdant with moss. (Jack Bryan)

logged. And because most of the new peoples chose to live and farm on the lowlands, few of these rain-shadow forests ever had a chance to regenerate. What forests there are sport only spindly second- and third-growth, but they are brightened in spring by the white bracts of the flowering dogwood, B.C.'s official emblem.

Also growing in this sheltered forest zone are two trees unique to the rain-shadow belt, the sinuous coppery-barked arbutus and the Garry oak. The arbutus is Canada's only evergreen hardwood, and it belongs to the same family as the madrona which grows along the Pacific Coast south all the way to Mexico. Its peeling red bark and handsome, glossy leaves, white flowers and red berries make it seem more suited to the tropics. The oak, which thrives on the driest and rockiest of sites only on southern Vancouver Island and the Gulf Islands, is at the northern limits of its range here

and grows only very slowly, its gnarled limbs and craggy bark often thick with moss. Because it likes the level areas of the coastal plain, today the most populated, here it is a tree struggling for survival.

Most of the shrubs and flowers of the wet forest also grow in the dry areas, but there are others that can be found only in the rain shadow — camas, brodiaea, satin flowers, erythroniums, both pink and white varieties, shooting stars and blue-eyed mary. Broom and gorse, both brought over from England, have run wild and spread their spring gold generously.

Farther up the mountain slopes, the character of the coast forest changes as the soil becomes thinner, the slopes generally steeper and colder. Trees of the mild, wet lowland are gradually superceded, at lower elevations in the north than in the south, by alpine fir, yellow cedar and mountain

hemlock. This forest in turn thins out to huckleberry and mountain-ash country, becoming colder and stonier until it reaches the tree line.

The tree line varies in elevation according to latitude: it is far higher in the south than in the north because it is controlled mainly by snow load. Above, the alpine country is frozen and snow-covered for a good eight months of the year, and the thin, rocky soil can support only limited vegetation. Immediately above tree line are alpine meadows, bright with carpets of flowers in July, where a few tough, stunted junipers and firs also grow. Higher, the meadows give way to patches of tough heather; higher still, only small creeping plants and lichens can survive. At the topmost levels, the land is barren rock and ice and snow, very much an Ice-Age landscape.

Forests play a critical role in the life of British Columbians. While at first look it seems that this role is purely local and economic — the forest industry traditionally has accounted for two out of every three jobs in the province — on closer scrutiny a greater importance emerges. It has been determined that forests influence the world climate. Forested land — which the world is losing at the rate of almost half a million acres a year — collects and returns to the air ten times as much moisture as bare earth, and at least twice as much as grassland. In addition, trees absorb carbon dioxide from the air and give out oxygen, which all living creatures on earth need. In the last century the amount of carbon dioxide in the atmosphere has diminished by fifteen percent and this loss is said to be accelerating, creating a detrimental "greenhouse" effect which increases world temperatures.

Careful management of the B.C. forests on a true sustained-yield basis will mean better health for the B.C. economy — and the world.

Above right — *Spanish moss hangs like draped tinsel on the dead lower limbs of a tall Douglas fir.* (Bob Herger — Photo/Graphics)
Right — *Mushrooms and other fungi grow well in the rain-forest environment. This is a bracket fungus.* (David Hatler)

54

Forests cover the valleys and all but the highest of British Columbia's mountains.
(Douglas Cowell)

Wildlife

More than seventy percent of all the species of birds and mammals that breed in Canada are found in British Columbia. The shores, forests and mountains of the western slope provide a diversity of habitats, refuges in some cases for wildlife that elsewhere in the world is threatened with extinction. The west coast is also home to several species found nowhere else in North America, or nowhere else in the world.

The B.C. Coast is known among naturalists for the great number and diversity of its birds. Woodland birds include woodpeckers, Steller's and Canada jays, thrushes, towhees, band-tailed pigeons, wrens, kinglets, flycatchers and tiny bushtits. Some birds have been introduced from other continents. Of these, the English skylark is at home in the fields around Victoria, the crested mynah from China is found in large numbers around urban Vancouver, and the California quail calls in the dry Gulf Islands. Except for a few strays occasionally sighted in the Puget Sound area of Washington State, the skylark and the mynah can be found nowhere else in North America.

The birds of sea and shore are more numerous and perhaps more noteworthy than those of the land. Many of

Left — *Pigeon guillemots are common colony-nesters on isolated sea cliffs.* (David Hatler)
Right — *The bald eagle is numerous along coastal inlets and islets, its numbers in B.C. estimated at between 10,000 and 15,000.* (Lyn Hancock)

Tufted puffins nest in burrows excavated into the soil of grassy slopes and headlands, mostly along the west coast of Vancouver Island and on the Queen Charlottes. (Lyn Hancock)

Right — *Black oystercatchers with their red beaks and pink legs are common residents of the coast. They are so named because they pry open shellfish with their bills.* (Lyn Hancock)
Below left — *The great blue heron, expert fisherman of freshwater streams and ocean shallows.* (David Hatler)
Below right — *Black brant migrate along the coast, stopping to feed in favorite beds of eelgrass.* (B.C. Government)

these are only visitors, pausing en route between their northern nesting grounds and southern wintering spots; some spend the winters here; some come here to nest; others are permanent residents. Among the latter, the most impressive is the bald eagle which is still numerous along coastal inlets and islands, though elsewhere, except for Alaska, it is extinct or on the decline. B.C.'s eagle population is estimated at between 10,000 and 15,000.

The birds are big, up to fourteen pounds, with six-foot wingspans, and they build huge nests in the tops of tall trees along the shore. The largest nest so far measured was nine feet across and more than four feet thick, its weight estimated at almost a ton. Nesting pairs return to the same site year after year, each time adding a new lining of seaweed and evergreen boughs. Because of the weight of the nest, suitable trees are hard to find: they must be tall and stout, at least ten feet in diameter and thus at least four hundred years old. Unlike Alaska, B.C. does not protect eagle habitat, and as more of the shoreline is denuded by clear-cut logging, destruction of suitable nesting trees could bring a decrease in the eagle population.

Eagles are principally shoreline scavengers, feeding on dead or dying marine life, but they also prey on live small birds and other creatures such as fish, crab and abalone. In the fall, they feast on the carcasses of spawned salmon in coastal streams. Eagles are sometimes so locally numerous at spawning time that a score or more will be perched in one waterfront tree — like large black and white flowers.

The peregrine falcon, extinct in many parts of the world because of hunting and pesticide damage, is holding its own in isolated havens along the coast, particularly in Juan Perez Sound in the Queen Charlotte Islands, which supports the highest breeding densities in the world. Even so, peregrine population is low: in 1980, estimates for the Queen Charlottes were given at fewer than 250. The peregrine nests on isolated cliff ledges and trees and feeds on live birds, mostly murrelets and auklets in summer, small ducks in winter, all of which are locally abundant. The swiftest of all the raptors, the peregrine strikes its prey on the wing in dives that reach speeds of more than two hundred miles an hour.

Top — *Brandt's cormorant, on nest, displays its bright blue throat patch only in the breeding season.* (David Hatler)
Above — *Snow geese in the tens of thousands wing south from Siberia and Alaska to rest in the salt marshes of the Reifel Island refuge, south of Vancouver.* (Gunter Marx — Photo/Graphics)

Cormorants nest in raucous colonies on the cliffs of tiny Mitlenatch Island, a nature reserve in the Strait of Georgia. (Bob Sutherland — Photo/Graphics)

61

Above/Right — *Mandarte Island, an Indian reserve near Sidney on Vancouver Island, has been designated an ecological reserve because of its nesting populations of glaucous-winged gulls, cormorants, guillemots, oystercatchers and puffins.* (Lyn Hancock)

On the west coast of Vancouver Island, isolated cliffs safe from predators are preferred nesting grounds for Brandt's cormorants. They lay three to six eggs. (David Hatler)

Falconers prize the bird above all others and it commands a high price on the international market. Poaching is still a concern.

Only a few of the shorebirds are residents: most are migrants, nesting in the Arctic and wintering in the south, like the snow geese and Canada geese that pass through from Alaska and Siberia, pausing in huge flocks to feed and rest in such places as the Fraser delta and Alberni Inlet marshes. Trumpeter swans, once considered endangered, winter in estuaries and lakes along the B.C. Coast. Huge rafts of surf and common scoters, Barrow's and common goldeneye ducks, coots, loons and grebes are commonly seen in the winter even close to urban areas, bobbing in bays off Vancouver's Stanley Park and around Victoria.

Perhaps the B.C. Coast is most famous among bird-watchers for its large numbers of seabirds which nest in col-onies on remote rocky islets. Most of these birds are pelagic, living far out at sea and coming to shore only to nest and rear their young. Some build nests on rocky ledges, other at the ends of long burrows which they tunnel into the forest floor. The southern Queen Charlotte Islands, because of their isolation and proximity to rich oceanic feeding areas, are one of the most prolific seabird nesting areas along the whole Pacific Coast. Here can be found eighty percent of B.C.'s nesting storm petrels, both Leach's and the fork-tailed, which burrow into the soft soil of the spruce forests under the thick cover of salal. Here, too, are seventy-five percent of B.C.'s ancient murrelets and fifty percent of its tufted puffins and Cassin's auklets. There are more of these auklets in B.C., about a million, than anywhere else in the world. Two other birds, the horned puffin and the common murre, breed only in the southern Queen Charlottes.

Canadian Galapagos

Sunset casts an amethyst glow behind the snowy San Cristoval Mountains of Moresby Island, second largest island of the Queen Charlottes. (Jurgen Vogt — Photo/Graphics)

The isolated Queen Charlotte Islands, sixty miles off the coast of British Columbia, have been likened by scientists to the Galapagos Islands because of the great number of distinctive plants and animals found there. Six land mammals, three birds, several insects, fish, mosses, liverworts and flowering plants are found on the Charlottes and nowhere else in the world. In addition, there are several plants whose relatives occur in such scattered locations as Scotland, the Himalayas, Borneo, the Alps, Japan and the Faroe Islands, but nowhere else in the New World.

All these species, scientists say, must have required at least ten thousand years to evolve on the Queen Charlottes, but ten thousand years ago, Ice Age glaciers smothered all of B.C., making life impossible and interrupting the natural evolutionary process. This apparent contradiction is neatly solved by the relatively new theory of Ice Age refugia. Lack of a continental shelf off the Charlottes' steep west coast likely made it very difficult for snow to amass into glaciers. Instead, it is argued, snow on the slopes simply sloughed off into the relatively warm sea, baring the ground so a few hardy species could survive.

Ancient pollens and plant fossils bear out this

theory, proving that at a time when the rest of B.C. was icebound, forests were growing in at least part of the Charlottes. Here survived a few plants and animals — including the world's largest black bear — adapting to the cold, breeding and evolving, while elsewhere whole populations simply died out or retreated from the ice. When the ice melted, plants and animals, with different evolutionary histories, moved back.

The islands' wildlife is interesting for more than the Ice-Age survivors. Isolation since the Pleistocene Era has led to the evolution of different species on different islands of the archipelago, exactly as Charles Darwin found on the Galapagos. Darwin noticed differences in finches and turtles; on the Charlottes, the clues to evolution are found in deer mice and sticklebacks.

The unique flora and fauna combined with the rich cultural heritage of the Haida Indians have made the unspoiled southern part of the Queen Charlottes a candidate for national park status. On south Moresby, if park status is granted, an intact coastal ecosystem will be saved from the logger's ax, ensuring the continuation of genetically diverse forms of life and allowing scientists to study the equilibrium of the islands' complex ecological web.

Spotted cougar kits explore the roots of a giant cedar on Vancouver Island. Young can be born at any month of the year. (Lyn Hancock)

Once common throughout the western half of North America, the cougar today can only be found in wilderness areas where it lives chiefly on deer. It is still fairly common throughout the B.C. Coast where it is known to swim from island to island. This one seems to be going fishing. (Lyn Hancock)

Other colony nesters are the pigeon guillemot, common throughout the coast, and the rhinoceros auklet. The latter, so named because of the small, hornlike tuft of feathers that grows above its bill during breeding season, is currently on the increase in B.C., probably because of the rich marine food supply.

Some of the nesting islands are in southern waters. In the Strait of Georgia, Mandarte Island off Sidney and Mitlenatch Island off Campbell River are both well known. On Mandarte, more than two thousand pairs of glaucous-winged gulls nest along with cormorants, guillemots, black oystercatchers and the occasional tufted puffin, the latter rare in the south. Mitlenatch is a provincial reserve, with naturalists on duty in the summer to guide visitors and guard the nests.

Near Tofino on the west coast of Vancouver Island, Cleland Island, another of B.C.'s ecological reserves, has nesting colonies of gulls, guillemots, storm petrels, oystercatchers (the world's densest population), rhinoceros auklets and puffins. Petrels and auklets return to their burrows only at dusk, to feed their young or exchange egg-sitting duties, and fly off again at dawn.

The most spectacular of the nesting islands lies thirty miles off the northern tip of Vancouver Island. Tiny Triangle Island, the outermost of the scattered group of Scott Islands, has a nesting population in the hundreds of thousands composed of thirteen different species including about 360,000 Cassin's auklets.

Also numerous along the coast is the marbled murrelet, a small, inconspicuous bird which was once the subject of a great natural history mystery. While it is common along the shores of the Pacific from Alaska to central California, no one could discover where it nested, despite a most active search. Now it is believed that the murrelet nests in the tops of tall Douglas firs, many miles inland, and brings its fledglings to the coast in June, though to date only four nests have been found, two in Alaska, one in California and one in Siberia.

Its relative, the ancient murrelet, which breeds in such huge numbers in the Queen Charlotte Islands, is noteworthy in that its newly hatched young, without ever being fed in the nest, manage to clamber out of the burrow and fall down to the sea, where they immediately begin to feed themselves on plankton and small crustaceans.

Mammals

Because the west coast is isolated by the mountains from the rest of Canada, unique subspecies of some of the mammals have developed here, particularly on the islands. The Columbian black-tailed deer, relative of the interior mule deer, is found only west of the Coast Mountain divide. Logging has favoured this species because it creates the open spaces and tender new growth that deer prefer, though on northern Vancouver Island, deer numbers are decreasing. Found only on Vancouver Island is a species of cougar (another frequents the mainland), a small remnant herd of Roosevelt elk, and a large-skulled species of black bear. Also unique to Vancouver Island is a dark brown marmot, a creature of the alpine meadows. Not recorded at all until 1910, and not seen again for twenty years, the Vancouver Island marmot is considered an endangered species: a search of the island's central mountains in 1983 counted only 165 animals. A government marmot management plan is now in place and 500 acres of prime habitat have been given to the province by MacMillan Bloedel; it seems that the marmots may now survive.

Several unique subspecies of mammal have also evolved, through insularity and inbreeding, and perhaps because of Ice Age refugia, on the Queen Charlottes. These include a black bear, the largest in Canada, marten, otter, weasel, shrew and several white-footed mice. Other species common on the mainland are not found at all on the islands: grizzly bear, cougar, wolf, mountain goat, fisher and flying squirrel.

Whales, porpoises, dolphins, seals and sea lions live in the waters off the B.C. Coast. Of the whales, the black and white orca or killer whales are the most numerous, travelling in pods of two hundred and more. Robson Bight in Johnstone Strait, recently recommended as an ecological reserve, has been called one of the best areas in the world

Continues on page 77

One of the smaller denizens of the forest, the Pacific tree frog has a large voice. (David Hatler)

Left — *Black bear watches for fish in shallow waters off the west coast of Vancouver Island.* (David Hatler)

Above — *Bear tracks in the muddy sand of a river estuary.* (B.C. Government)

Left — *A unique species of dark brown marmot is making its last stand in the vastness of the Vancouver Island mountains. A recent marmot management program seems to have stabilized its declining numbers.* (B.C. Government)

Right — *Found only west of the Coast Mountain divide, the black-tailed deer is numerous along the coast, though it was unknown on the Queen Charlottes until its introduction.* (David Hatler)

Below — *A raccoon scavenges in the kelp beds along the west coast of Vancouver Island near Tofino.* (David Hatler)

Larger and lighter in color than the California species, the northern or Steller sea lion is gregarious and polygamous and spends much of its time hauled up on rocky shores or islets such as these in Fife Sound. (John Ford)

The waters off the B.C. Coast support large numbers of whales, and whale-watching is becoming a popular activity. Passengers on the M.V. Gikumi get a close look at a killer whale, or orca. (John Ford)

Above — *Two killer whales breach in perfect harmony in Johnstone Strait.* (John Ford)

Left — *At Robson Bight on the northeast coast of Vancouver Island, killer whales congregate to mate and to rub their skins on the smooth rocks.* (John Ford)
Above — *Gray whales migrating off the west coast of Vancouver Island allow tourists to approach, even to pet them.* (John Ford)

Return of the Sea Otter

At the beginning of the eighteenth century it is estimated that at least 150,000 sea otters lived on the North American west coast from California to Alaska. Much in demand because of their soft, fine fur, the friendly little animals were mercilessly hunted, their pelts traded by the Indians for white man's goods and sold to the lucrative markets of China and Europe. By 1911, when the animals became protected under U.S. law, their numbers had dwindled to between one and two thousand, most of them in Alaskan waters. In British Columbia they were extinct by 1929.

Today, however, colonies of sea otters have been re-established and are thriving along the west coast of Vancouver Island, immigrants from Alaska. The first transplants arrived from Amchitka Island, a wildlife refuge that became a nuclear testing site. Twenty-nine otters were taken from Amchitka in 1969, before the blast, and transported by air to Checleset Bay south of the Brooks Peninsula, very near the spot where Canada's last recorded otter was shot. All arrived alive but in miserable condition after a long, interrupted journey, and it was not known how many survived. A year later, forty more otters were shipped south from Prince William Sound, but of these only fourteen arrived alive after the rough sea journey.

A third transplant operation, conducted in 1972, was more successful. The captured otters were first placed in floating pens for observation and only the forty-six fittest were airlifted out to Checleset Bay, one of B.C.'s protected ecological reserves. Here they were transferred again to floating pens and watched to make sure they were fit enough to survive in strange territory. All forty-six were later released.

Scientists did not really know how successful the re-stocking program was until 1984, when a three-day boat and aerial survey of the area brought good news. The transplanted sea otters were more than holding their own. They were on the increase. A total of 345 otters were counted, about 60 percent in the release area of Checleset Bay and the rest in a large colony at Bajo Reef, 40 miles southeast.

Protected today under the Federal Fisheries Act and classified as an endangered species in B.C., sea otters have a beneficial effect on their environment because they eat the red sea-urchins which destroy the kelp beds. And healthy offshore kelp beds mean healthy populations of herring and other small fish necessary in the marine food chain.

British Columbia's sea otters are few compared to populations in Alaska and Eastern Russia of 120,000, in California of 2,000. But they have made a good start and their numbers are burgeoning. Biologists are so happy with the successful transplant that they want to repeat the procedure, this time off the west coast of the Queen Charlotte Islands, where sea otters were once numerous.

The sea otter, hunted to extinction along the B.C. Coast for its fur, now lives in transplanted, protected colonies on the west coast of Vancouver Island. (Terry Willis — Photo/Graphics)

Right — *Harbor seal sports a fine set of whiskers.* (Vancouver Visitors Bureau)
Far right — *Northern sea lions bob in the sea off Long Beach, Vancouver Island.* (David Hatler)
Below — *Harbor seals bask on a rocky islet off Saturna Island in the Strait of Georgia.* (John Ford)
Below right — *Northern sea lions on the rocks in Fife Sound.* (John Ford)

Above — *Largest of all the seals, the male elephant seal is so named because of its strange overhanging proboscis.* (David Hatler)
Left — *Killer whale and its young spy-hop off Vancouver Island's misty shores.* (John Ford)

Continued from page 68
to see large numbers of these magnificent creatures. Gray whales can be seen cruising off the west coast of Vancouver Island and the Charlottes during their migration runs from the Gulf of Alaska to lower California, while the blue whale (the largest of all the world's whales), the humpback, the common finback and the sei whale can only occasionally be seen off the outer coast, more frequently in summer.

Closer to shore, the hair or harbor seal and the harbor porpoise frequent the bays and inlets. Here, too, in winter can be seen the northern sea lion, which spends the summer months in huge breeding groups on a few offshore islets. Largest colonies are in the Triangle/Scott Islands group off northern Vancouver Island, and the Kerouard Islands off the southern tip of the Queen Charlottes, the latter the largest sea lion rookery on the Pacific Coast, accommodating 800 adults and birthing an average of 300 pups.

Pacific striped dolphins winter off Vancouver Island. Dall porpoises often play in the wakes of West Coast ships. Sea otters, once common all along the west coast, were hounded to extinction in B.C. by the demands of the coastal fur trade of the eighteenth and nineteenth centuries. The species was recently re-introduced to the waters off the west coast of Vancouver Island, where the population today appears to be thriving.

Shore Life

Along the wave-washed edges of the land, the marine environment is one of the world's richest — a feast for the eyes and the palate. The Pacific Ocean has been temperate for a very long time, and its creatures have had ample opportunity to adapt and diversify. Along B.C.'s fractured and fragmented coastline they find a variety of habitat — mudflats, sand and pebble beaches and rocky headland — much of it sheltered from Pacific storms.

Rocky shores, which account for much of the coastline, are richest in seashore life. Animals are everywhere, on and under rocks, hiding in crevices or under seaweed, many of them brightly colored and strange of shape. Acorn barnacles,

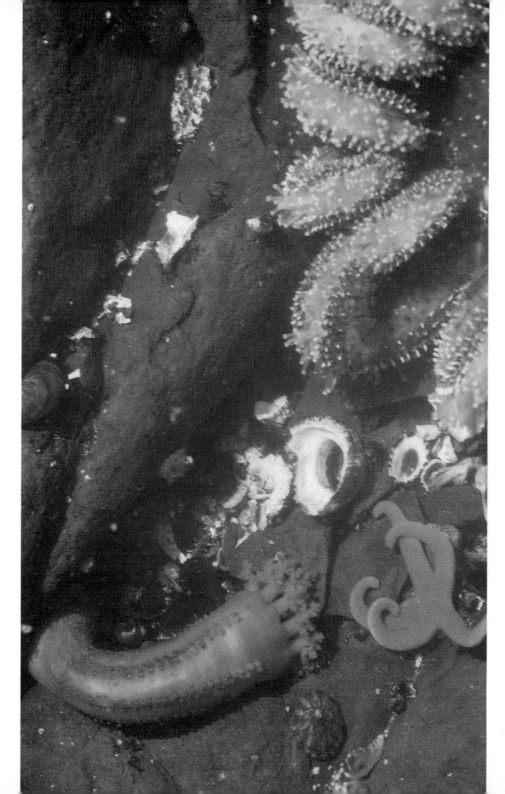

Opposite page — *Cruising killer whales breach in Johnstone Strait. The southern coast of B.C. supports the world's largest populations of this marine mammal.* (John Ford)

Left — *Tidepool still life: sunflower star, scarlet blood-star, orange sea cucumber.* (Gunter Marx — Photo/Graphics)

Above — *At Botany Beach near Port Renfrew, Vancouver Island, the rocky shore is pitted with tide pools. It is a good place for the study of marine life.* (Bill Staley)

periwinkles and limpets inhabit the dry zone of the upper beach. In the midzone live mussels, many different snails and limpets, gooseneck barnacles and hermit crabs, pill bugs and isopods. Farther down the beach, exposed only by the lowest tides, grow many kinds and colors of seaweed, their exotic names aptly descriptive of form: Turkish towel, cup-and-saucer, eyelet silk, sea staghorn, seersucker and feather boa. Here, too, are multi-hued sea stars — B.C. waters are home to the world's greatest variety, including the giant sunflower star, a yard across and with up to two dozen arms — delicate-looking anemones hiding their predatory nature behind lovely flower forms; prickly sea urchins, cup coral, nudibranchs, snails, spider crabs, sea cucumbers, squirts and chitons. Chitons are ancient armour-plated creatures that curl up like pillbugs when disturbed. Along the B.C. Coast they are larger, more abundant and more conspicuous than anywhere else in the world. The largest is the rubbery gumboot chiton, a foot long, looking exactly like the sole of a fisherman's boot.

Wherever the encroaching waves have worn the shoreline down into sea-level ledges, low tide reveals eroded rock hollows or tidepools where creatures that normally live unseen, submarine lives are exposed briefly. The tidal shelf at Botany Beach near Bamfield, on the southwestern shore of Vancouver Island, provides one of the richest and most extensive tide-pool displays of marine life, well-stocked aquaria that change their contents with the tides. Even fish, small, jellyfish and baby octopus can become trapped here. The Pacific octopus is the largest in the world, growing to one hundred pounds, with an arm spread of eighteen feet. Another rich intertidal habitat is Burnaby Narrows, on Moresby Island in the Charlottes.

Beaches of cobblestone or gravel are the places to go for clams. Littlenecks, known as steamer clams, are abundant, although the accidentally introduced Japanese variety now outnumbers them. Butter clams, the most important commercially, and the more deeply buried large horse clams and even larger geoducks, the largest burrowing bivalves in the world, can also be found here. Geoducks, which grow to eight pounds and more in weight, are harvested by divers

Below left — *Close-up of a purple sea star.* (Bill Staley)
Below right — *Chiton, abundant along the B.C. Coast, dwarfs a yellow sea star.* (David Hatler)

Above left — *The Pacific octopus is the largest of its species in the world. Here a small one is stranded in a tide pool.* (Bill Staley)
Above right — *Green "petalled" sea anemone waits for its dinner.* (Bill Staley)
Right — *Scuba diver fishes for urchins off Vancouver Island.* (Lyn Hancock)

who sluice them out of the mud of shallow bays with hydraulic jets.

Sand beaches appear on the surface to be barren except for flotsam cast up by the waves along the tide line: a litter of shells and seaweed, long ropes of bullwhip kelp, or the odd stranded jellyfish. But buried below the hard low-tide sand are sand dollars, snails, worms and three kinds of clam, the razor, tellen and sand. The tasty Dungeness crab lurks in shallow pools, hiding in beds of eelgrass, while shrimp swim in the shallows at the sea's edge.

Oysters can be found in protected bays, usually where seawater salinity is reduced by freshwater drainage. The native oyster is diminishing possibly due to pollution, but it is being replaced by the larger Japanese variety imported in 1905.

The Pacific Ocean is a rich feeding ground for many kinds of fish, particularly salmon, herring, halibut, dogfish and cod. Five species of salmon are found: chinook, coho, sockeye, pink and chum. Chinooks are the largest — a six-year-old may weigh eighty pounds or more — and the most sought after by sport fishermen, while sockeye is the most commercially valuable.

Left — *Sea palm, mussels and barnacles, Vancouver Island.* (David Hatler)
Top — *Sea urchins and sea stars, exposed by the retreating tide, provide a feast for a foraging raccoon.* (Lyn Hancock)
Above — *Eelgrass and bull kelp, west coast Vancouver Island.* (David Hatler)

Below — *Horse clam, one of several edible varieties found along the coast. This clam is tough, but excellent for chowder.* (David Hatler)

Right — *A mess of purple sea stars, exposed by the tide. West Vancouver shore.* (Bill Staley)
Far right — *Sockeyes spawn in several west coast rivers. Some of the large Fraser runs spawn in unbelievable numbers in the gravel beds of the Adams River near Chase in the B.C. interior.* (Fisheries Council of B.C.)

The First People

It is still generally believed that mankind first came to America from Siberia only about twelve thousand years ago, crossing the Bering Strait in the waning days of the last Ice Age, when the sea level was still low and the continental shelf was exposed. The dry interior regions of Alaska and the Yukon were never glaciated and on these tundra plains lived caribou, deer, horses, camels and hairy mammoths, some of which had also crossed from Siberia on the land bridge. Fossilized remains of these Ice Age beasts are fairly common, but until recently no evidence had been found of the ancient human beings who hunted them.

In the last twenty years, however, the established parameters for North American prehistory have been drastically upset. Archeologists have discovered among the rich deposits of animal fossils in the Yukon's Old Crow Basin unmistakable traces of man that date back at least 80,000 years to the Ice Age before last, and possibly to 150,000 years. First evidence was a caribou leg bone toothed at one end to form a fleshing tool, found in 1966 among the fossilized bones of Ice Age animals. Many other artifacts, most of them expertly chipped from fresh mastodon bones, were later unearthed from undisturbed old river gravels.

Left — *In the legends of the Haida, man was born from a clamshell, helped by a raven. Magnificent sculpture by artist Bill Reid commemorates the legend and stands in the University of B.C. Museum of Anthropology.*
(University of B.C.)
Right — *Bella Coola mask.*
(University of B.C.)

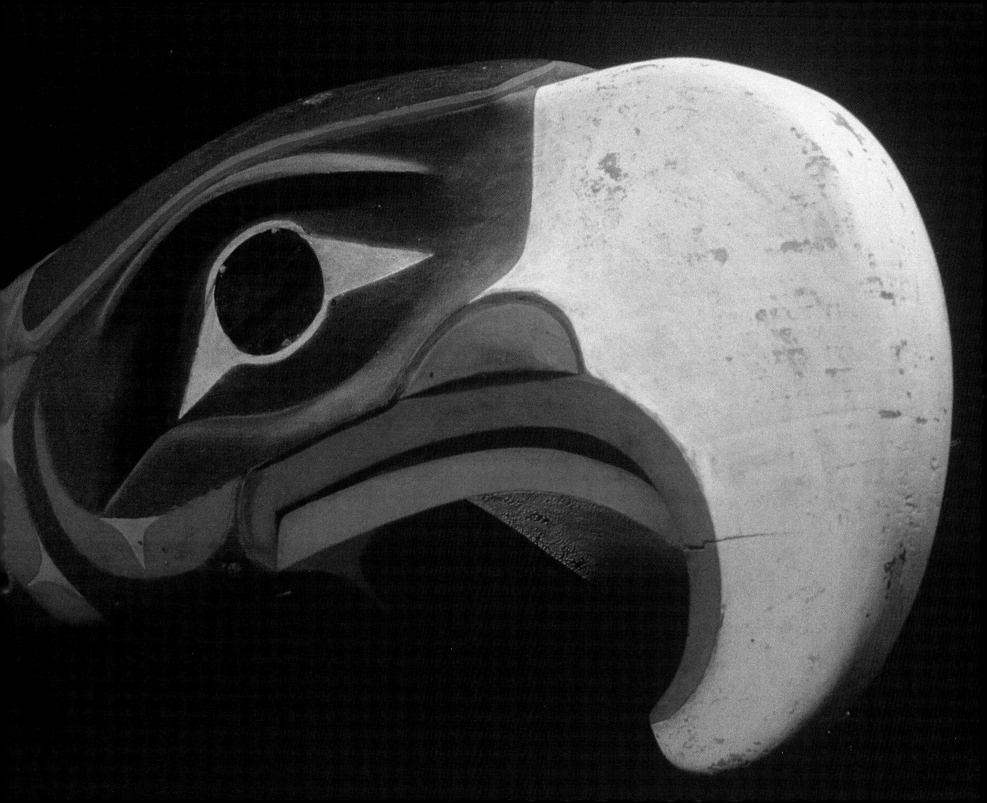

Right — *Weathered totem on Effingham Island.* (David Hatler)
Far right — *Haida memorial pole, carved in 1961 by Bill Reid and Doug Cranmer, stands outside the UBC Museum of Anthropology.* (University of B.C.

Left — *Totems at Skidegate, Queen Charlotte Islands.* (B.C. Government)
Top — *Salish basket, pre-1916.* (University of B.C.)
Middle — *Tsimshian wooden soul catcher, circa 1860.* (University of B.C.)
Bottom — *Tlingit horn comb, circa 1900.* (University of B.C.)

Found, too, were the jaw and thin teeth of a domestic dog and traces of a very ancient encampment, complete with the charcoal of a campfire. So far, only one human bone has come to light, the lower jaw of a twelve-year-old child.

These ancient "Bone Age" men, well adapted to the cold, probably followed the herds of now mostly extinct animals across the landscape of western Canada, moving ever southward until they colonized all of North and South America, a scenario previously assumed to have taken place much later, when the last Ice Age was on the decline. Archeologists say that man probably could not have survived on the ice cap itself, so must have travelled south down the coast, where the climate along the exposed continental shelf was tempered by the relatively warm ocean. Others believe the migrants came down an ice-free north-south corridor which opened between the Cordilleran ice of the western mountains and the continental ice of the plains during one of the several warmer epochs. In both areas, the cataclysmic aftermath of the Ice Age — rising sea levels and flooding rivers — has left few traces of their passage.

In British Columbia the earliest traces of man, found in the Peace River area of the extreme northeast, date back only to 10,000 years. On the coastal slope, archeological remains are younger still, dating from after the last Ice Age, and signs indicate that these people came not from the north, but from the south, immigrants to the new lands that the retreating ice laid bare. Ongoing archeological work may one day provide a clearer account of the comings and goings of ancient man in western North America, the forebears of today's native peoples.

The Indians of the B.C. Coast belong to five different language groups and seven distinct tribes: Coast Salish, on both sides of the Strait of Georgia; Nootka (or West Coast People), on the west coast of Vancouver Island; Kwagiutl, both sides of Queen Charlotte Strait; Haida, on the Queen Charlotte Islands; Bella Coola, at the head of Dean Channel; Tsimshian, around the Nass and the Skeena, and the Tlingit of the north coast.

When the first white explorers arrived on the coast in the eighteenth century, estimates of Indian population ranged

Right — *Cemetery gates at Alert Bay, northern Vancouver Island, frame view of mortuary poles.* (Marin Petkov) — Photo/Graphics
Below — *Totems at the Queen Charlotte museum, Tanu.* (Bob Sutherland — Photo/Graphics)
Below right — *Totem at University of B.C.* (Bill Staley)

Right — *Women in ceremonial button blankets and cedar bark await opening of U'Mista Cultural Centre at Alert Bay, northern Vancouver Island, in 1980. White headdresses are ermine skins.* (Vickie Jensen)

Stone Enigmas

Petroglyph at Thorsen Creek near Bella Coola. (B.C. Parks)

Cut into wave-washed boulders, sandstone ledges and cliffs at many locations along the British Columbia coast are prehistoric Indian carvings or petroglyphs. Assumed to be the work of ancestors of present-day Indians, these carvings are of uncertain age (though undoubtedly ancient) and equivocal meaning. But they are links, nevertheless, with the continuing human presence along B.C.'s sparsely populated coast, and they may one day provide clues to the origins and migration routes of the first peoples.

Some of the petroglyph sites are enormous, whole slabs of rock or beaches full of decorated boulders; some are only a single motif, miles from any others. Many of the carvings are of human figures, mostly curiously stylized with exaggerated heads and staring eyes; others are clearly of animals, birds, fish and even insects; some are stars or suns, all representations, perhaps, of the real world. There is also a great deal of fantasy — strange spirit figures, sea monsters, dragons, circles and spirals and mazes that belong to a supernatural world, a world in which prehistoric man was deeply enmeshed.

Most anthropologists believe that the petroglyph sites were sacred places of power, where the priests or

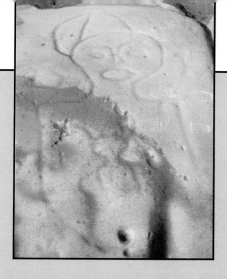

Petroglyph of human figure on rock beside the West Coast Trail, Pacific Rim National Park. (B.C. Parks)

Petroglyph of sailboat beside West Coast Trail must date from after the Spaniards arrived on the coast. (B.C. Parks)

shamans communicated with the spirit world. Stylistically they fall into several groupings, and some are today etched far deeper into the rock than others, suggesting they were done by different groups of people some centuries apart. But in all the sites, from the Alaska border to the Columbia River, anthropologists can find several common links and trace a single cultural affinity.

Petroglyphs have been found near Metlakatla, on Pitt Island in Grenville Channel, and on Roberts Point near Prince Rupert. There are many sites in the Bella Bella area — at Meadow Island, Return Passage, Manu Lake, Elcho Harbour, the Bella Coola canyon and the mouth of the Nootasum River. Only one site has so far been found on the Queen Charlottes, near Skidegate, but Vancouver Island has many, mostly on the east coast. The best known of these is at the provincial Petroglyph Park near Nanaimo, where a great slab of decorated rock is on display. At Port Neville, another huge knob of granite has glyphs in three distinct styles. At Kulleet Bay in Ladysmith, hidden in the forest some thirty feet from shore, a sandstone slab contains twenty-one individual figures, while across the bay is the solitary figure of a god.

The islands that dot the Gulf of Georgia are similarly rich; there are known sites on Quadra, Cortes, Hornby, Saltspring and Gabriola, some of them discovered only recently, buried under inches of earth. At Cape Mudge on the southern tip of Quadra Island the beach used to be literally strewn with petroglyph boulders, at the mercy of wave action and submerged by the high tide. The Cape Mudge Indians have recently moved the boulders off the beach into a covered enclosure in Yaculta Village, to protect them from further erosion — and from vandalism.

Thoughtless people have, over the years, destroyed many of these ancient carvings, obliterating possible clues to an understanding of our past. All petroglyph sites are protected by the B.C. Heritage Conservation Act, which prohibits even the taking of rubbings without a special permit. (Covering the carving with soft paper or cloth, then rubbing over it with crayon, produces an eye-catching reverse image of the petroglyph. The pursuit was becoming so popular that some of the more accessible carvings were in danger of being literally rubbed away.)

Petroglyphs along the coast, whatever their age or meaning, provide a bridge into the unknown past, a link with a forgotten prehistory that can only enrich our lives.

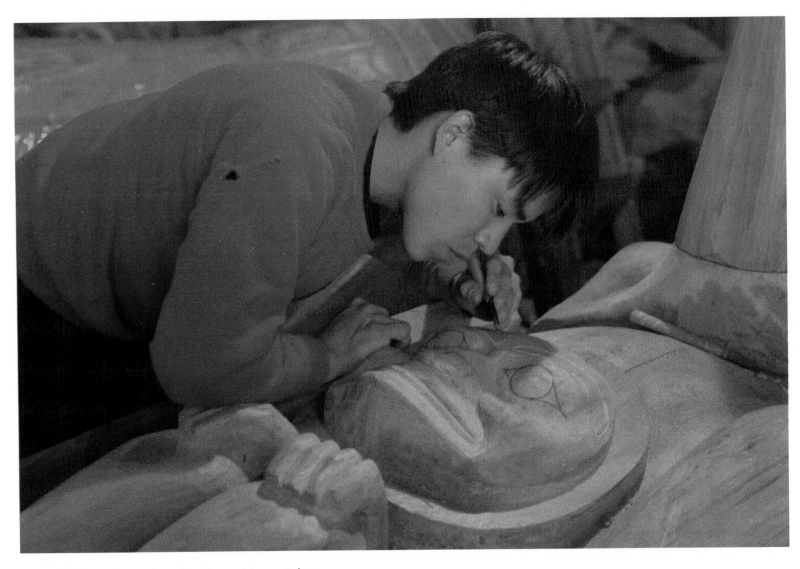

Isaac Tait, Nishga carver, works on moon face on totem erected at
Native Education Centre, Vancouver, in 1985. (Vickie Jensen)

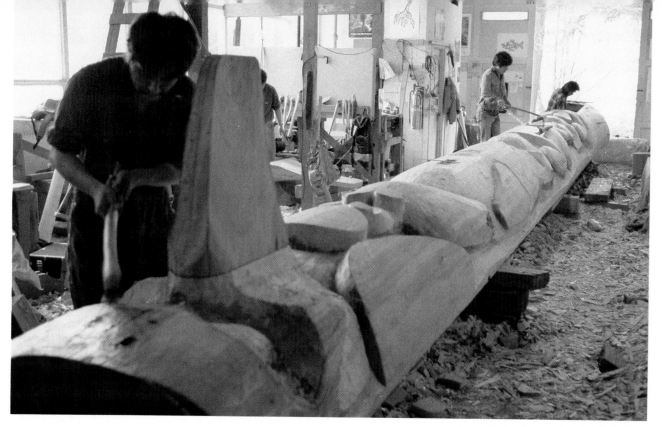

Above — *Indian craftsman repairs a Native canoe. The Haida built large, sturdy deep-sea boats that enabled them to hunt whales.* (Vickie Jensen)
Above right — *Norman Tait and crew work on 42-foot totem for Native Education Centre, Vancouver.* (Vickie Jensen)

from 80,000 to 125,000. Coast Indians were affluent, the richest nonagricultural society the world has ever seen, for they lived in a temperate land well endowed with natural resources.

All the coastal tribes shared an economy based on super-abundance: of salmon which migrated yearly in colossal numbers up all the coastal streams; and of cedar, whose tall, rot-proof timbers were easily cut and carved, and which grew in dense stands along the shore. Theirs could have been a culture of feast and famine, for the food glut was narrowly seasonal, but they developed such excellent technologies for catching and preserving their major food supply that they had plenty all year, with surplus to lay away or trade. While the tribes of the interior were nomads, moving ceaselessly in search of food, the tribes of the coast lived in permanent villages and in the leisure of their affluence they developed complex social, artistic and religious traditions.

They were technically competent. They could fell and split huge cedars for their large communal houses, carve out whole trunks for canoes, make waterproof capes and mats from shredded cedar bark, knot fishing nets of nettle fibre, weave waterproof baskets of spruce roots, and carve bone fishhooks and harpoons. And they made these everyday things beautiful, richly decorated with carvings, paint and embellishment that reflected tribal legends and proclaimed each family's hereditary rights and privileges. They acted out their spiritual and cultural beliefs in intricate ceremonies and dances that required whole sets of nonutilitarian objects such as masks and rattles.

When the first Europeans arrived on the coast in the mid-1700s, native arts were flourishing, for the Indian traditions, including the gift-giving feast of potlatch, encouraged and supported artistic creativity. Artists and carvers were honored specialists, esteemed for their talents. The fur trade brought more wealth to the coastal tribes and their art industries accelerated. European imports — iron knife blades and hatchets — made carving faster and more precise, and there was a lively demand among the sailors and traders

Far left — *Welcoming ceremonies for the 1985 Asian Festival in Vancouver. Lead canoe is Kwagiutl, with Simon Dick standing by the bow, dancing. Other canoes bring Nishga carvers from the Nass River.* (Vickie Jensen)
Left — *Raising the totem at the Indian Cultural Centre.* (Phil Hersee)

Left — *Natives traveling by traditional canoe carry their craft ashore en route to the Asian Festival.* (Phil Hersee)
Above — *The old Indian traditions and regalia are today being passed down to new generations. Both old and young participated at the Asian Festival.* (Phil Hersee)

for souvenir items. For a brief while, the arts of the Northwest Coast flourished as never before.

But then began a swift decline, not of Indian arts alone, but of the whole underpinnings of Indian culture. European diseases decimated the native population, and European missionaries did their best to destroy not only their traditional beliefs but their way of life. Anthropologists and art collectors carted off boatloads of tribal heritage treasures — masks, rattles, dance screens, even totem poles — to faraway museums. Government legislators banned the spirit dances and the potlatch, curtailed fishing and hunting, instituted in some areas a system of land reserves, and insisted on educating Indian children in European ways, often in missionary schools far removed from native communities. The southern Kwagiutl continued to hold some of the forbidden ceremonies in secret, but elsewhere along the coast the ancient culture and traditions were dying. Some, like the ancient Tsimshian, were irrevocably lost.

William Taylor, director of Canada's National Museum of Man, has described the Northwest Coast art tradition as "one of mankind's greatest artistic achievements, ranking with the outstanding traditions of China and Japan, tribal Africa, pre-Columbian Middle America and the European Renaissance." It could not be allowed to die.

And it didn't. The University of British Columbia and the B.C. Provincial Museum were probably the main instigators of a revival movement that began around 1950, received fresh impetus when the potlatch ban was revoked in 1958, and today is vigorous and burgeoning. Around two hundred Indian men and women now earn their living full-time as Northwest Coast artists, some of them as carvers for the Provincial Museum in Victoria. Here much of their work entails replicating old masks and dance regalia for loan to native communities which are reviving the potlatch and other ceremonies, and re-instilling a fierce sense of native pride.

Robert Davidson, a Haida carver of international acclaim, is seen as a key figure in this artistic revival movement. In the 1960s he carved a forty-foot totem pole for the village of Masset in the Queen Charlotte Islands, the first to be

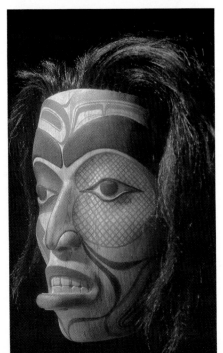

Above — *Norman Tait at the totem-raising ceremony in Vancouver wears the eagle helmet he carved. The eyes are abalone. For Native festivals, craftsmen sometimes "borrow back" the ceremonial items that were commissioned by museums in Vancouver, Victoria and other communities.* (Vickie Jensen)
Left — *Haida wooden mask, made in 1970.* (University of B.C.)
Right — *Totem-raising ceremony at Alert Bay graveyard, northern Vancouver Island, a tradition still carried on today in Native communities along the coast to commemorate the death of a chief. Tony Hunt carved the totem in 1976.* (Vickie Jensen)

Right — *The potlatch is a strong cultural event among the Kwagiutl in Alert Bay, northern Vancouver Island. Such gatherings, outlawed for many years, may last twelve hours. Traditional names, songs, dances and masks are all inherited and are displayed and used at the potlatch ceremonies. The events are private and only those personally invited may attend.* (Vickie Jensen)

Above — *At Haida village, bleached logs on the beach and house poles proudly in place seem to symbolize the unity of the Native environment, as seen through the eyes of a small boy. To add to the Native atmosphere, a raven keeps watch.* (Jurgen Vogt — Photo/Graphics)

Right — *Potlatch was held by William Cranmer at Alert Bay when he was given a name and ceremonial property by older chief. Potlatch goods piled up on display are payment to the witnesses of the event.* (Vickie Jensen)

Right — Indian children on beach at Klemtu eat their lunch of barbecued salmon on plates made from devil's club leaves. (Lyn Hancock)
Far right — Coast Indian salmon barbecue on beach at Alert Bay in front of the U'Mista Cultural Centre. Salmon is barbecued in the smoke of an alder fire. (Vickie Jensen)

Right — Agnes Cranmer skillfully prepares a Nimpkish River sockeye for barbecuing on the beach in traditional Indian way. (Vickie Jensen)

erected there in ninety years. To honor the occasion, the villagers held a potlatch, with traditional songs and dances. This event kindled an interest in traditional art among young natives of this and other communities along the coast, and helped to foster the resurgence of native identity.

Most West Coast Indian artists today are skilled duplicators of traditional masks, crests, totem poles and other items. And some are beginning to recapture the essence of the art form, its strong intermingling with the world of spirits. The old motifs are growing and changing, as art must do to remain vital and relevant.

Changing, too, is the Indian perception of themselves. Long subjugated in a white man's world, Northwest Indians today are taking new pride in their ancestry and heritage. Their children are being taught the old languages, myths and dances of their tribes and the traditional community ceremonies, including the once-outlawed potlatch, are becoming once again a part of their lives.

The native Indians are also claiming ownership of huge areas of tribal land — the whole of the Queen Charlotte Islands, for example — that they say were taken from them without consent or compensation. Settlement of Indian land claims along the coast, as in the North, will have far-reaching effects on the Indians themselves and on the economy of the whole province.

101

Discovery and Exploration

Although there remains the intriguing possibility that England's Sir Francis Drake sailed to the coast of British Columbia as early as 1597, it seems more likely that the Spanish were the first European visitors. Juan Perez in the ship *Santiago* left San Blas, Mexico, in January, 1774. His mission: to sail north to latitude 60 degrees and to take possession of the land. There was a sense of urgency to his mission. Russian explorers Vitus Bering and Aleksi Chirikov had reached North America in 1741, and news of the abundance of sea otters off the coast of Alaska had sparked considerable Russian trade in the North Pacific, an area that Spain considered hers on two accounts. A papal bull of 1493 had given to Spain all of the New World except Brazil, and in 1513 Balboa had crossed the Isthmus of Panama and laid Spanish claim to all the Pacific lands.

By mid-July Perez and the Santiago had reached latitude 51 degrees 40 seconds and headed east in search of land. They caught their first glimpse of British Columbia, the west coast of the Queen Charlotte Islands, on July 18, saw their first canoe load of singing Haida Indians on July 20, and traded trinkets for dried fish. They sailed on to the northwest tip of the Queen Charlottes, trading with other natives for

Captain James Cook sailed the B.C. Coast in 1778 in search of the Northwest Passage. Trading with the Indians for the furs of the sea otter, he opened the eyes of the world to the maritime riches of the Northwest Coast.
(B.C. Archives)
Right — *Modern beach fires burn in the dying light of a summer sunset at Vancouver's Spanish Banks beach. Its name commemorates the meeting between Captain Vancouver and the Spanish commanders Galiano and Valdez in 1792.*
(Jack Bryan)

furs, then on July 23 turned south for Mexico, dropping anchor briefly on August 8 off the mouth of Nootka Sound on the west coast of Vancouver Island.

A second Spanish expedition was sent out the following year to complete Perez' mission, this time of two ships, the *Santiago* and the *Sonora*. They became separated; the *Santiago* turned back in the cold and fog somewhere off the west coast of Vancouver Island, but the *Sonora* made it all the way to latitude 58 degrees, well into Alaskan waters.

Neither of these expeditions had sent a party to shore. The first European foot to tread on British Columbia soil was British. In 1778 Captain James Cook, with his ships the *Resolution* and the *Discovery*, came to the Pacific in search of the elusive Northwest Passage around the top of North America. After discovering the Hawaiian Islands, Cook crossed the ocean to the coast of today's Oregon, then sailed north. On March 29 his ships entered Nootka Sound, at first unaware that the Spaniards had anchored close by four years earlier. Indians in canoes welcomed the ships and next day they traded, offering skins of sea otter and other animals in return for iron goods. Cook moved his ships into a cove on Bligh Island and his crew came ashore to undertake necessary repairs, setting up a tent camp on Observatory Rock. Cook later toured the area, calling in at the nearby Indian village of Yuquot, or Friendly Cove, which he found offered superior anchorage, and making note of the dense stands of enormous trees. Cook stayed nearly a month, by which time the sailors had acquired a number of furs that later they were to trade in China for small fortunes.

Cook himself was subsequently killed by natives in Hawaii, but even before his journals were published, word of the plentiful supply of otter furs on the North Pacific Coast had leaked to maritime entrepreneurs. The rush was on.

The first fur trader to reach Nootka was James Hanna in the brig *Harmon,* which sailed from China in 1785. He stayed just over a month and collected 560 sea otter pelts, which brought him 20,600 Spanish dollars in Canton. From there on, trading ships were regular visitors to the B.C. Coast, and Friendly Cove in Nootka Sound became their harbour of destination. Most stayed only briefly, but when English

Early white explorers and fur-traders were usually given a friendly greeting by the Natives, who came out to their ships in canoes very much the same as this Haida canoe arriving for Vancouver's Asian Festival in 1985. (Phil Hersee)

Engraving of an artist's impression of Nootka Sound made in 1798,
during the time of Spanish settlement. Notice the large cross.
(B.C. Archives)

trader John Meares sailed into the cove in 1788, he bought some land from Chief Maquinna, constructed a dormitory and supply depot, and set his men to work building a sloop. Present at the launching of the *North West America,* the first ship built on the coast, was the first of several fur traders from the United States of America, Captain Robert Gray, who was later to discover the Columbia River.

This flurry of fur-trading activity by the British and the Americans in the south, the Russians in the north, finally stirred Spain into action. Still believing herself legal owner of all the Pacific lands of the New World, Spain sent two warships north from Mexico to assert sovereignty. Landing at Friendly Cove, Don Esteban Martinez formally took possession of the land in the name of King Carlos III and built two forts, San Miguel and San Rafael, to guard the entrance of Nootka Sound. Two British trading ships that later came into the sound were looted and seized, the boats and crew sent off as prisoners to Mexico.

The Spanish base at Nootka was abandoned that same year on orders from the Mexican viceroy, but then a new viceroy ordered it to be built again and placed under the command of Don Francisco de Eliza. Early in 1790, Eliza refurbished Fort San Miguel for his garrison of seventy-five troops, built barracks, supply buildings, an ambitious governor's residence, a church and a hospital. Eliza also sent out expeditions to explore and take possession of more of the coast.

Few people in England knew or cared about Nootka, a small indentation on the unexplored coast of a distant land, but when they learned of the seizure of British ships and seamen they were outraged. The British government prepared for war. Spain hastily capitulated with the Nootka Convention of 1790, which guaranteed restitution of seized property and allowed Britons to trade anywhere in the Pacific except within ten miles of Spanish-occupied territory.

The presence of the Spanish fort and settlement at Nootka did not discourage the fur traders. By the summer of 1791, a dozen ships, most of them American, were trading along the B.C. Coast, though they avoided conflict by staying away from Friendly Cove. At the end of the season, Captain Gray

and the crew of his ship, the *Columbia,* decided to winter in Clayoquot Sound and in a sheltered cove on Meares Island they built Fort Defiance and began construction of the sloop *Adventure.* There were now Spanish, British and American buildings on the B.C. Coast.

By one account, no fewer than thirty foreign ships visited the coast in 1792. One of them was the *Discovery,* captained by George Vancouver, come to survey the northwest coast of North America with his companion ship, the *Chatham.* Several were Spanish, the schooners *Sutil* and *Mexicana* and the frigate *Aranzazu;* their mission: to explore as much of the coast of the new country as possible and claim it for Spain.

In April Juan Francisco de la Bodega y Quadra, commander of Spain's west coast navy, arrived at Nootka to rendezvous with Captain Vancouver for the formal conclusion of the Nootka Convention. Vancouver, however, was busy exploring and mapping the new coast. He sailed into Puget Sound, then north into the Gulf of Georgia, taking possession in the name of Britain of all the lands that bordered the gulf. He missed the Fraser River mouth, but named and landed at Point Grey in today's Vancouver, then explored and named Burrard Inlet, Howe Sound and Jervis Inlet. Returning south, he met the Spanish *Sutil* and *Mexicana* anchored off Vancouver's Spanish Banks and invited their commanders, Galiano and Valdez, to join him in a joint expedition to northern waters. They sailed together into Desolation Sound, around Cape Mudge, and up Bute Inlet into Johnstone Strait. Here, Vancouver went on ahead of the Spaniards into Queen Charlotte and Fitzhugh sounds, where a trading vessel informed him that Quadra was waiting for him at Nootka.

On August 28, the *Discovery* and the *Chatham* hove to anchor in Friendly Cove. Vancouver fired a thirteen-cannon salute to the Spanish flag, and Quadra diplomatically fired thirteen rounds for the British. But the negotiations that followed were not so easy. All Quadra would surrender was the tiny cove and plot of land upon which John Meares had built his house, while Vancouver would accept all or nothing. During the weeks of punctiliously diplomatic negotiations,

Oil painting of Captain George Vancouver who, in his ship Discovery, *surveyed the coast in 1792 and '93 and gave his name to a city, an island and a fur-trading fort which is now Vancouver, Washington.* (B.C. Archives)

Engraving of Alexander Mackenzie, of the North West Company of fur-traders from Montreal, who made the first overland journey to the B.C. Coast in 1793, leaving his name and the terse details of his trip painted on a rock in Dean Channel, left. (B.C. Archives)

Friendly Cove in Nootka Sound today, still accessible only from the sea. The church (see spire, foreground) was built on the spot of the original Spanish church. (B.C. Government)

Vancouver and his officers were hosted graciously at Quadra's house, dining off solid silver and eating the finest of fare. His crew were treated to fresh vegetables from the Spanish gardens and newly baked bread. Despite social pleasantries, the deadlock could not be resolved and the matter was referred back to the home governments. Quadra returned to Mexico; Vancouver, after sending a message back to London by way of China, to Hawaii for the winter. Later, a revised Nootka Convention saw the settlement at Friendly Cove relinquished by Spain; the Indians tore down the buildings to get the iron nails, and rebuilt their own longhouses along the shore. Britain had to agree not to maintain a permanent post at Nootka, though the Union Jack was allowed to fly over the parcel of land that Englishman Meares had bought.

Vancouver returned to his survey of the coast the following year (1793), the same year that Alexander Mackenzie, a young employee of the North West Company of fur traders from Montreal, reached the Pacific after a momentous overland expedition from Fort Chipewyan. Mackenzie and nine voyageurs travelled down the Peace, the Parsnip and the Fraser rivers, then west over the stickleback ridges of the Coast Mountains by way of the West Road River, 6,000-foot Mackenzie Pass and the Bella Coola River to tidewater at the head of Burke Channel. Mackenzie tried to explore the shoreline, but was turned back by hostile Indians. He left the record of his passage painted in grease and vermilion on a rock in Dean Channel. Vancouver had been in that very vicinity only a few weeks previously. What a pity that these two great adventurers did not meet.

Vancouver's meticulous mapping and Mackenzie's bold journey were immensely important to the history of B.C., ensuring as they did that the future of this great unknown land lay in British hands. Vancouver died in England in 1798, but the published account of his Voyage of Discovery was ample evidence, not only of his prodigious work, but of the justness of future British land claims to the B.C. Coast. Mackenzie's Journals were finally published in 1801. Both books did much to increase world awareness of the New World's northwestern reaches. Too, they made the young United States of America realize that if their new country was ever to extend to the Pacific, more than the minimal presence of American traders off the coast was needed.

Accordingly a United States army expedition led by Captains Lewis and Clark set out overland from St. Louis for the Pacific. They arrived at the mouth of the Columbia in November, 1805, and raised the Stars and Stripes above a hastily built Fort Clatsop, where they spent the winter. They made no proclamation of American sovereignty but, like Mackenzie, left a record of their visit posted on the fort wall.

That same year the Canadian North West Company, led by Simon Fraser, began to extend its fur-trading activities west of the Rocky Mountains. From a new base at Rocky Mountain Portage on the Peace River, Fraser followed Mackenzie's route up the Parsnip River, then turned aside to found Trout Lake Post, later known as Fort McLeod, the first permanent white settlement in B.C. Fraser was later to establish Forts Fraser and St. James in the country he called New Caledonia. What the British needed for these inland trading posts was a supply route from the Pacific. The first company to find one would have control of the Pacific inland fur trade.

The most promising route was the Columbia River. Two men from the North West Company were given the mission to find its inland passage and to follow it to the sea. In 1808 the energetic Simon Fraser set off from near today's city of Prince George down a major river that he believed to be the Columbia. After two months of hair-raising adventure, including the negotiation of boiling rapids and sheer rock canyons, he arrived at the Pacific far north of the Columbia's mouth. He had instead written his name across the map of future British Columbia, discovering and descending the river that was later to bear his own name.

The other man to go in search of the Columbia was David Thompson, who crossed the Rocky Mountains in the south and in 1807 established a fortified trading post, Kootenae House, right on the banks of the Columbia River near today's Invermere. Thompson did not suspect that this stream, which here flows almost due north, was in fact the river of his search. Nor was he in any apparent hurry to complete his mission of discovery. For the next four years he dallied,

trading with the Kootenay Indians and building new trading posts. When he finally pushed downstream to the river's mouth in the summer of 1811, it was too late: the American Pacific Fur Company under John Jacob Astor was already there. The Stars and Stripes, not the Union Jack, commanded this strategic position and the seeds of a split sovereignty had been sown.

The maritime fur trade continued for the next twenty years in the face of increasing Indian hostility and decreasing numbers of sea otters. From about 1835 on, with the otter fast becoming extinct, the emphasis of history shifts to the inland fur-trading network and to the increasingly adamant claims by both Britain and America to possession of the northwest coast. Following the War of 1812 (in which Fort Astoria was first sold to the North West Company, then taken as a booty of war, then given back again), America and Britain had agreed to a period of co-occupation in which each was free to trade and establish settlements in the disputed lands. Nearly all of the trading and settlement was done by the British Hudson's Bay Company (which had earlier merged with the North West Company), but in the 1840s an increasing number of American settlers arrived by way of the Oregon Trail. American expansionism increased; tension between the two countries mounted. The border question would have to be resolved.

Britain wanted the line drawn along the north shore of the Columbia River, enclosing today's Washington and parts of Idaho and Montana within British domain. In America the extremists wanted everything up to the then-Russian boundary of 54/40 — and were prepared to fight, while others conceded that a fairer settlement would be the extension of the 49th parallel which formed the international boundary through the prairies. While many historians concede that the British had an excellent case for their claims, by prior discovery and settlement, in 1846 a weak administration in London, anxious to avoid war, settled for a boundary line along the 49th parallel with one concession: that the line dip south to include all of Vancouver Island. The shape of British Columbia had finally been determined.

Gold

While it was the fur trade that first beamed the spotlight of history onto the British Columbia Coast, and the trading posts that formed the nuclei of settlement, it was gold that brought the province into the mainstream of world events. Until gold was found in the Fraser River, the west coast of British North America, known as New Caledonia, belonged in effect to the Hudson's Bay Company, which had leased exclusive trading rights on the mainland and had been made "true and absolute lords and proprietors" of Vancouver Island. Accordingly, most of the residents were employees of the company, though a few independent settlers had been brought out from England to satisfy crown requests for colonization.

The rich Fraser River and Cariboo gold rushes so overshadowed the first gold discovery in B.C. that it has been almost forgotten. This took place in 1850 at Gold Harbour, on the west coast of the Queen Charlotte Islands, where HBC traders found an extensive deposit. Unfriendly Haida Indians prevented the men from working the claim immediately, and word of the discovery spread. Convoys of ships, most of them American, set out for the Charlottes with parties of prospectors. The HBC returned to protect its claim, a thin seam of

Fort Victoria, Hudson's Bay Company headquarters and capital of a tiny outpost colony of the British Empire, was overwhelmed by an influx of miners from San Francisco in 1858. (B.C. Archives)

Left — *It was the discovery of gold on the Fraser River and farther inland that precipitated the opening up of the province to trade and settlement. Miners traveled by boat up the river as far as Yale, then continued by primitive trails. Ox teams hauling long loads to the upriver diggings were a familiar sight at Yale. (B.C. Archives)*

gold ore, in places twenty-five percent pure, which extended for some eighty feet. As it turned out, this seam was the only gold on the islands; prospectors searched in vain along the shore and inland, then sailed away.

Eight years later gold was discovered, again by HBC men, in the sands of the Thompson River near its confluence with the Fraser. Again word of the find leaked south, and again most of the first prospectors were Americans, galvanized into action by a large shipment of gold which arrived at the San Francisco mint from British America. In April, 1858, 450 men, fresh from the tag end of the California gold rush, sailed north in the side-wheeler *Commodore*. They leaped ashore at tiny Fort Victoria, the HBC headquarters and capital of the colony of Vancouver Island. The three hundred inhabitants of the staid British outpost, most of whom had heard nothing of the gold finds, gaped in amazement, half afraid they were being invaded. And in a way they were. Boatloads of miners arrived almost every week for the rest of the year, and the result of this influx was to transform Victoria into a bustling town, full of new buildings and businesses. Most of the newcomers stayed only long enough to pick up supplies and arrange transportation to the new Eldorado, but some came to stay, opening stores and saloons; veterans of the American gold rush, they knew these were surer ways to get rich. By the end of the year the fort community had a population of more than three thousand residents, with sometimes as many as ten thousand transients encamped nearby. But throughout all the excitement it retained a fair modicum of British dignity; there were churches, a girls's school, a uniformed police force, one paved street, two newspapers and even a cricket club.

On the B.C. mainland, men swarmed up the Fraser. Those who could afford the twenty dollar fare sailed upriver as far as Fort Hope. Others travelled by canoe, on horseback or on foot, panning for gold on all the sandbars and tributaries, hacking rough trails into the hinterland, and building flimsy camps beside the river. They pressed farther and farther inland, trading for supplies at HBC posts where astonished factors now reckoned their profits in gold dust instead of furs.

Thousands of miles away in civilized London, the British

government suddenly woke up to the fact that the obscure wilderness land of New Caledonia, leased to the HBC for a song, was a valuable possession. They hastily revoked the HBC privilege and declared the land west of the Rockies to be a new crown colony. Queen Victoria herself chose its name, British Columbia.

The inauguration ceremony took place in the rain at Fort Langley on November 20, 1858. Matthew Begbie became the colony's first judge and James Douglas, head of the HBC and governor of Vancouver Island, left the company to become British Columbia's first governor. On his own initiative Dougas had imposed a five dollar license fee on the miners. Now, with the help of Royal Engineers from the Boundary Survey, he organized the colony's first police force, collected import duties, appointed gold commissioners to regulate the miners, and surveyed new towns at Fort Hope and Fort Yale. He was also instructed to open the new lands for settlement. People of any nationality except Chinese were allowed to pre-empt one hundred sixty acres each as long as they cleared it, fenced it and built a homestead. With this incentive, many of the miners traded their pans for ploughshares and settled down to tame the wilderness. Settlements grew up around the HBC posts of Forts Langley, Hope and Yale, at Port Douglas at the north end of Harrison Lake, at Lytton at the mouth of the Thompson, and at New Westminster, the new colonial capital, on the north bank of the lower Fraser. Civilization was encroaching fast.

Gold was abundant in the Fraser. In 1858 alone an estimated total of 106,000 ounces was taken out, worth today about thirty-five million dollars. It was found all along the

Early view of Yale, head of navigation on the lower Fraser River. Paddlewheel steamers came upriver to this point, then supplies and men went overland. (B.C. Archives)

Hell's Gate, the narrowest neck of the Fraser Canyon, was a formidable obstacle for road and railway alike. (B.C. Archives)

The S.S. *Beaver*

First steamship along the northwest coast, the S.S. Beaver, photographed in Vancouver in 1888. She arrived in 1835 and served the coast well for more than fifty years. (B.C. Archives)

First steamship to ply the waters off the British Columbia coast was the S.S. *Beaver*, launched in London, England, in 1835 for the Hudson's Bay Company. She arrived at Fort Vancouver on the Columbia River in April the following year. Thereafter, she was sent north on trading voyages between company posts in the mostly still uncharted territory of "New Caledonia." She was a sturdy little ship, one hundred feet long and twenty broad, with an elm keel and English oaken timbers. Propelled by paddlewheels thirteen feet in diameter and powered by two thirty-five-horsepower side-lever engines, the *Beaver* quickly became the HBC workhorse because she proved far superior to sailing ships when it came to maneuvering in the long, labyrinthine inlets that make up the B.C. coast. Fueled by wood and plying a shoreline thickly forested down to tidewater, she nevertheless carried sails for emergency power.

For twenty years the *Beaver*, armed with brass cannon, traded up and down the coast from Johnstone Strait to the Nass River. Her large crew, thirty-one, was partly for defense and partly to keep the little

The Beaver *was wrecked at Prospect Point near today's Lions Gate Bridge, Vancouver, in July, 1888. She had served her final years as a towboat.* (B.C. Archives)

steamer supplied with wood. Large woodpiles were cached at convenient locations all along the steamer's regular route.

In 1862, the *Beaver* was commissioned by the Royal Navy for survey duties along the coast, and for eight years she helped in the charting of the tortuous coastline. By this time she had burned through five new boilers and been refitted several times. Her original timbers, however, were still stout enough to withstand a grounding on vicious Race Rocks at the entrance to Victoria harbour.

When she finished her service with the navy she was sold to private interests and refitted as a towboat, her principal business, towing lumber ships to Burrard Inlet, coal ships to Nanaimo, and transporting supplies to coastal logging camps. In 1883 she holed on a rock

at First Narrows (site of today's Lion's Gate Bridge, at the entrance to Vancouver harbour), but was raised and beached at the new town of Granville and later repaired and refitted as a passenger ship. But in 1888 the old paddlewheeler, bound for Thurlow Island with a load of logging supplies, ran aground at Prospect Point and there she was left to disintegrate, stripped and looted by curio hunters and at the mercy of the fierce currents. For years a landmark, the *Beaver*, herald of the steam age in a country in some respects still in the Stone Age, slipped gradually into the sea. By 1894, all traces had vanished.

Recently, however, local divers Fred Rogers and Eddie Seaton retrieved her anchor and parts of her machinery, which are now on display in Vancouver's maritime museum.

river above Fort Hope, though the gravel bars in the canyon were the richest. There was plenty of violence and mayhem and trouble with the Indians, though the firm hand of British law kept it all reasonably well under control. Since much of the trouble was caused by liquor, the colonial administration prohibited its sale to Indians and made each saloon keeper buy a hefty six hundred dollar license.

The focus of the Fraser gold rush moved gradually upriver as lower bars became exhausted. In 1860, miners reached Fort Alexandria in the "upper country," where gold took the form not of fine flour but thick flakes and even small nuggets, and was found not in the Fraser but in the Quesnel and Cariboo rivers, in Keithley and Harvey Creeks. Prospectors surged in, looking for the mother lode. Some struggled over the Snowshoe Plateau and down into a new valley, that of Antler Creek. Here lay the bonanza, a supply of gold so generous that a singe pan yielded seventy-five to a hundred dollars. A midwinter stampede over the snows of the high plateau, and the Cariboo gold rush was on! By 1861, Antler Creek was a town of sixty houses, a store, saloons and gambling establishments. Prospectors roamed farther afield; the creeks of Williams, Lowhee, Grouse and Lightning became overnight sensations; gold of unbelievable abundance being found in the river gravels and in nearby clay deposits. Wells Fargo alone shipped $1.4 million in Cariboo gold in 1861, a figure that in today's dollar would be closer to $30 million. The staid *London Times* conservatively estimated the total take of the 5,000 miners that year to be almost $7 million, or $150 million today.

The Cariboo was rich — richer, some said than California. Miners poured in, even though the land was snow-covered for six months of the year and the journey from the coast far and arduous. Provisions were hard to come by and enormously expensive. Many prospectors abandoned their hopes on the trail and returned home penniless. In the spring of 1862, construction began on a wagon road from Yale, the head of navigation on the Fraser, through the tortuous Fraser Canyon and into the Cariboo. It was a slow and difficult job, taking a full three years to complete, but it was a major factor in opening up the interior of B.C. to settlement.

In August of 1862, Billy Barker struck pay dirt fifty-two feet down in the glacial gravels below the canyon of Williams Creek. This was the richest claim of all. Land adjacent to Barker's was immediately staked by other miners, and from their shacks the town of Barkerville was born. The epitome of the Cariboo fantasy, it was one long street crammed with hotels and saloons; a church at one end, an opera house in the middle, Chinese opium dens and joss houses, respectable businesses and families and hurdy-gurdy girls. With gold dust in the air and ever the hope of more, Barkerville in its heyday lured men north as never before in the lusty heyday years from 1863 to 1865, and as Barkerville thrived, the coastal settlements of New Westminster and Victoria lost their frontier images and became respectable cities.

The scarlet and gold stagecoaches of the BC Express carried 14 passengers at breakneck speed up the Cariboo Road, covering the distance from Yale to Soda Creek in a mere 48 hours. Horses were changed every 13 miles. This restored coach is at Barkerville. (Liz Bryan)

The end of the Cariboo Road was the loud and lusty gold camp of Barkerville, named for Billy Barker, an ebullient Cornishman who struck a rich gold seam nearby. The town was one long street of hotels, saloons, gambling dens, bawdy houses and other establishments of dubious repute, but at one end was beautiful St. Saviour's Church. The Barkerville heyday lasted for only two years, from 1863 to 1865, though the town lingered on. It was almost a ghost town in the 1950's when the B.C. Government restored it as a historic park. (Liz Bryan)

The first train to cross Canada on the new Canadian Pacific Railway steamed into Vancouver on May 23, 1887, to an uproarious reception. Today, Waterfront Station of the city's spanking new Skytrain overlooks the site. (B.C. Archives)

Railways

It was gold that first brought large numbers of people into British Columbia, and gold that provided the impetus for the first roads and built most of the new communities. But it was the coming of the Canadian Pacific Railway to Burrard Inlet in 1885, first to Port Moody, then to the deeper harbour at the mill town of Hastings, that shifted the focus of settlement. At the end of the rails, a new city, Vancouver, quickly outgrew both New Westminster and Victoria to become virtually overnight the commercial and manufacturing centre of B.C., the third-largest metropolis in Canada and an important world port. In 1908, a second transcontinental line, the Grand Trunk

Pacific, laid tracks from Edmonton, Alberta, to Fort George (now Prince George) and west to a new port of Prince Rupert near the mouth of the Skeena. Other railways also pushed into the western wilderness: the Canadian Northern Pacific built down the Thompson and Fraser rivers to New Westminster; the American Great Northern battled with the CPR for first access to the coal mines of Crowsnest Pass and the silver, gold and copper mines of the southern interior; the CPR later extended its line to the Okanagan Valley and over the Coquihalla Pass to Hope; the Pacific Great Eastern (now the B.C. Railway) built north from North Vancouver to Prince George and beyond. From 1881 to 1911, the years of railway expansion, B.C.'s population grew to around 400,000, of which 100,000 lived in the new city of Vancouver, a pattern which has persisted.

117

Settlement and Resources

The history of settlement along the British Columbia Coast corresponds with definite wave patterns of resource exploitation. First the sea-otter fur trade, then the gold rush, then the other resources of the sea — whales, fur seals and salmon — and of the land — coal, copper and iron, and always, the great wealth of the forests.

One by one these resources were discovered, used, misused and, in some cases, used up. Where resources were to be found, people came to settle and make a living. The maritime fur trade was an exception: it prompted exploration but little permanent settlement, for the sea otters were soon almost wiped out; they were probably never very numerous. The gold of the Fraser, which brought in hordes of immigrants and created many of B.C.'s first towns and roads, was soon played out, though it lasted for half a century in the interior. Whales were hunted almost to extinction, their carcasses rendered at shore stations such as Whaletown on Cortez Island, Cachalot and Coal Harbour on Vancouver Island, and Rose Harbour in the Queen Charlottes. These communities were, like the whales, not long-lasting. In the years of plenty an average of 1,200 whales a year were taken off the B.C. coast; in 1942 the catch had dwindled to around

Left — Putting in the undercut, possibly at Myrtle Point, around 1924, when there were still giant cedars in the forest. Notice the two men on springboards. (B.C. Archives)

118

In the early days of the logging industry, logs were hauled to water by teams of oxen, then floated down to the mills. (B.C. Archives)

150. Even so, the industry continued for another twenty-five years, finally coming to a close in 1967 when it seemed the big whales had all but gone from the coast.

Hunting for seals in B.C. waters was profitable (it supported a fleet of sealing schooners based in Victoria) but always wasteful. Foreign ships were barred from taking part in the easy land slaughter at the seal rookeries in Alaska, and it was impossible to retrieve more than half of the animals slain at sea. An international treaty in 1911 banned pelagic sealing in the North Pacific, but by then the herds that once had numbered in the millions had shrunk to less than 150,000.

Coal was discovered as early as 1835 along the east coast of Vancouver Island. When the steamships and railways of a later era created a firmer demand, the mines around the Hudson's Bay Company post at Nanaimo became big business. For a hundred years, coal was the economic mainstay of the island export economy and the Nanaimo mines in particular supported large settlements of miners and tradespeople. When the coal seams were exhausted, the mines and some of the towns closed down. Iron deposits on Texada Island were first worked in 1885; later discoveries were made at Tasu on the Queen Charlottes and at scattered locations on Vancouver Island. Copper was found on Vancouver Island, in Howe Sound and on the extreme north coast at Anyox. Gold was mined for a while at Zeballos on the Queen Charlottes.

The early settlers knew that minerals were finite resources, that the mines, and the settlements based on them, would eventually shut down, and they would have to move on. But the Pacific was swarming with fish; salmon in unbelievable abundance choked the inlets and river mouths en route to spawning grounds in coastal rivers; huge schools

Left — *Men of the village of Sointula, a Finnish settlement on Malcolm Island off the north shore of Vancouver Island.* (B.C. Archives)

Below — *Settlers at Sointula were mostly fishermen, putting out to sea in simple dories.* (B.C. Archives)

of halibut and herring swam offshore, along with cod, sole and many other varieties. Surely this was an inexhaustible resource. No matter how many fishboats — gillnetters, seiners, trawlers and trollers — went after the catch, there always seemed to be plenty left. But while fishing still provides a livelihood for many B.C. people, the number it supports is drastically reduced.

The export potential of B.C. salmon had been realized early on by fur traders at Fort Langley, who had sent barrels of salt fish to Hawaii and Europe, but B.C.'s commercial fishery did not begin in earnest until the invention of the canning process. The first salmon cannery opened in 1867, at the mouth of the Fraser River, and others soon followed. Sockeye was the preferred species because it kept its color and texture better in the can; fishboats and canneries naturally concentrated in the sockeye grounds, which were particularly rich in Rivers Inlet and at the mouths of the Skeena and Fraser rivers. By the turn of the century seventy cannery settlements had sprung up along the coast.

Unlike the mining towns, these cannery camps were mostly seasonal, employing natives and large numbers of Chinese (who had come to B.C. to build the railways) only for several months each summer. But each became the nucleus for permanent settlement; homesteaders arrived to clear the woods and till the land, providing cannery workers with milk and fresh produce and augmenting their farm incomes by logging and cannery work.

By far the most important export industry, though second to gold in the early years, was (and still is) lumber. The first trees used by Europeans were cut to replace the masts on the eighteenth century sailing ships that visited the coast. Captain Cook himself used Douglas fir for this purpose when he put in at Nootka for repairs in 1778, and later trading vessels filled their holds, not only with furs but with ships' spars and rough timbers, which all the tall ships of the world's navies could use.

The Hudson's Bay Company built the first sawmill at Millstream near Victoria in 1848, and made the first export shipments of B.C. lumber to San Francisco and Hawaii. A second mill was constructed by private interests at Sooke,

Above — *McTavish Cannery, Rivers Inlet. The first cannery in B.C. opened in 1867 and by 1900 there were 70 operating along the coast.* (B.C. Archives)

Right — *Modern fish boats in Prince Rupert Harbour. Today the canneries have centralized to two locations, the mouth of the Fraser and Prince Rupert at the mouth of the Skeena.* (Fisheries Council of B.C.)

Cape Scott

Right — *Cape Scott today, scenic, deserted. The settlers gave up, leaving their farms and their clearings. Their trail, eighteen miles of track laboriously carved through thick forest, is today traveled only by hikers en route to the clean, lonely beaches of the Provincial Park.* (B.C. Government)

Left — *At a 1915 community fair, some of the Danish immigrants who settled remote Cape Scott, at the northwest tip of Vancouver Island, pose outside the schoolhouse.* (B.C. Archives)

Most of the early settlers on the British Columbia Coast chose land within easy reach of already established communities around the sheltered waters of Georgia Strait. But in 1896, a group of hardy Danes settled instead on one of the most exposed sections of the outer coast, Cape Scott, the rain- and wind-lashed northwestern corner of Vancouver Island. Here on meadows reclaimed from the encroaching sea and the marching sand dunes, they founded an independent colony, subsisting by farming and fishing and working in the salmon cannery at Rivers Inlet. Completely isolated from civilization except for a monthly steamer to nearby Fisherman's Bay, this little colony of ninety build cedar houses, a school and a sawmill, and even its own ship.

Despite heroic hard work, the colony did not survive. After three years the government refused to allocate any more land, and later reneged on the original agreement to grant homesteaders clear title to their lands. A promised road from Quatsino Sound up the San Josef River never materialized, and the fresh meat, vegetables and milk the farms produced could not easily reach market. The little colony was hampered, too, by the lack of large, sturdy boats for fishing halibut in the stormy offshore waters, but most of all by the extreme isolation.

One by one the families moved away, some to the head of Quatsino Sound, where they established a new settlement called Holberg after a famous Danish poet, some along the San Josef River, some on the inland side of the island at Hardy Bay (now Port Hardy). The land was opened to general pre-emption

and a new wave of settlers tried again to live in the wilderness, but the war of 1914 stopped development: many of the young men enlisted, and public funds that might have been used to build roads and wharves were diverted. Pre-emptors abandoned their holdings, settlements were deserted, the forest reclaimed the hard-won clearings and Cape Scott once again became a wilderness of wind and rain.

Then in the early days of the second World War, the Canadian government built an air force radar station at the tip of Cape Scott, and a seaplane base was established at nearby Coal Harbour in Quatsino Sound. At the end of the war, the Coal Harbour hangars were converted into a whaling station (closed in 1969), and the Cape Scott radar installations, barracks, messhalls and hospitals, were abandoned.

The small settlement at Holberg flourished as a logging town. In 1942 a floating logging camp was established in the inlet. It was a complete town, a quarter of a mile long, with houses and gardens, community hall, machine ship, store, fire hall, bunkhouses and hot and cold running water. At one time the largest floating town in the world, it lasted until 1956 when it was replaced by a new town on shore.

Holberg later became the site of a new, permanent air force radar base, and in 1971 base personnel decided to re-open the historic settlers' trail to Cape Scott. This eighteen-mile footpath, laboriously axed through the jungled rain forest and equipped with three overnight shelters, is today the only means of access to the marvellous sand beaches and wild coast of the cape, which has recently become a provincial park — 38,000 acres and 56 miles of shoreline left in its wilderness beauty. Only a few old cabins and clearings remain as mementoes of the pioneers.

and a third by the HBC at Nanaimo. This mill's purpose in part was to supply pit props for the Nanaimo coal mines. Other early mills were located at Port Alberni, at Mill Bay on Saanich Inlet and later at Chemainus. On the mainland, mills were built at the new gold-mining towns of Yale, Hope, Port Douglas and the new capital, New Westminster. These mills provided employment for many. Most of the early production was for local use, but it wasn't long before B.C. became a lumber exporter.

On the south side of what is now Vancouver's Inner Harbour was the mill pioneered by Captain Edward Stamp in 1865, later to be known as Hastings Mill. Stamp's timber reserve included the whole of today's Vancouver; the first cutting of ships' spars was made by foreman Jeremiah Rogers near his camp at Jerry's Cove, today's Jericho Beach. While Hastings Mill specialized in spars, Moody's Mill at the mouth of Lynn Creek, on the north side of the inlet, produced mainly sawn lumber. Owner Sewell (Sue) Moody boasted that his water-driven mill could produce more cheaply than any other on the coast. He built a second steam-powered mill adjacent to the original one in 1868, and this increased his capacity to around one hundred thousand feet per day, nearly double that of Hastings Mill. The mill town of Moodyville on the North Shore, with its seventy-five to one hundred workers and their families, quickly became not only the industrial hub but the social centre of Burrard Inlet. A wagon road, today's Kingsway, was put through from New Westminster to the south shore resort of New Brighton, and a ferry ran a triangular route between Brighton, Moodyville and Hastings Mill. Burrard Inlet bristled with the masts of sailing ships. In 1869, twenty-one ships loaded lumber, shingles and spars at Hastings Mill and twenty-four took on lumber at Moodyville; their destinations: South America, California, Australia, China, England and Hawaii. Each year more ships arrived, mostly to Burrard Inlet and Alberni Inlet on Vancouver Island, and it wasn't long before B.C. had some of the largest sawmills and pulp and paper mills in the world.

Supplying the mills were logging camps scattered along the dense shoreline forests north from Vancouver to Prince Rupert and the islands. Some of the camps were built on

Telegraph Cove, its buildings on stilts and joined by a wooden boardwalk, is typical of the many resource settlements that once dotted the B.C. Coast. (Lyn Hancock)

127

Old whaling station at Rose Harbour on the north coast of Khungit Island in the Queen Charlottes. The station once employed 150 men, was in operation from 1909 until World War II.
(B.C. Government)

floats so they could be easily towed to a new site when nearby forests were exhausted. Trees were hauled to tidewater along corduroy roads, first by trains of oxen, then by horses and later by rail. Then the logs were towed in huge booms to mills up and down the coast. Like the fish canneries, the logging camps and mills attracted settlement around them. They became towns, with stores, homes, schools, wharves, community halls, streetlights, theatres and ball parks.

At one time the isolated B.C. Coast was beaded with thriving communities, linked to the outside world of Victoria and Vancouver by steamship service which brought in mail and supplies and more settlers. In 1920 there were about eighty cannery and whaling stations, three mining towns and a myriad mill towns and logging camps along the coast, each worthy of a place on the map. For more than fifty years the Union Steamship Company was their lifeline. It called at all the settlements, often making as many as sixty-five stops between Vancouver and Rivers Inlet and as many again between Rivers Inlet and Prince Rupert.

Today most of these settlements and the people who lived in them are gone; the map is almost empty. First, the Indians abandoned their ancient, isolated village sites in favor of the new mining, logging and cannery communities. The whaling stations closed for good, Coal Harbour the last, in 1967. The fishing companies consolidated and the advent of larger refrigerated boats allowed the centralization of cannery operations at Steveston, at the mouth of the Fraser, and at Prince Rupert. Most of the other canneries closed. In the woods industry, logging camps became fewer, larger and more mechanized, and were serviced by company ships and planes. Minerals ran out, markets for lumber and pulp and paper dwindled, and mining and mill towns were deserted.

The Union Steamship Company phased out its once vital coastal service and the homesteaders, farmers, independent fishermen and loggers who might have stayed along the isolated, roadless coast could not survive without a lifeline. They, too, packed it in and went to the populous areas of Vancouver and Victoria. The B.C. Coast today is peppered with ghost towns, some like Ocean Falls, big and well-preserved and still living on hopes of better days; others small, a few crumbling cabins or factories or totems in the forest, testaments to hard work and broken dreams.

And as the trend toward centralization and urbanization grows, it seems doubtful whether the coast will ever become widely settled again.

The Cruel Coast

Canadian Life Guard vessel Camsell *patrols the west coast of Vancouver Island, even today one of the most treacherous coasts.*
(B.C. Government)

Mariners know it as "The Graveyard of the Pacific," and with just cause. The bones of hundreds of ships litter British Columbia's outer coast, victims of hidden reefs and rocks, of treacherous tides and currents, fierce storms that blow in from the Pacific or roar down the inlets, and endless banks of blinding fog. Uncounted human lives were lost with those ships. For all its beauty, it is not a kindly coast. For two hundred years it has brought disaster to all kinds of ships, from the small sailing schooners of the eighteenth century to the diesel-powered, steel-hulled vessels of today.

The grim litany of lost ships began as soon as Europeans first visited the coast, though there is no evidence that any early Spanish ships foundered here. The first wreck was probably that of the schooner *Lark* in 1786, lost with her crew of thirty-eight off Copper Island in the Queen Charlottes. Some of the other early ships were burned and their men murdered by Indians: the *Resolution* in 1793; the *Boston* in 1803; the *Tonquin,* blown up by a member of her own crew during an Indian attack in 1811.

Maritime traffic dramatically increased in the mid-nineteenth century, and the number of shipwrecks grew alarmingly. The lost ships were carrying miners to the B.C. goldfields and later to the Yukon and Alaska. They were inbound in ballast and outbound, their holds filled with coal, lumber and salmon. They were barques and brigantines, schooners and side-wheel steamers, tugboats and gunboats and luxury cruise ships, large ocean freighters and small ferries and fish boats.

The rugged west coast of Vancouver Island, in particular the stretch of smooth, virtually unindented and uninhabited land between Port Renfrew and Barkley Sound, is infamous in the annals of shipwreck. More than forty major wrecks, one for every mile of the shoreline, occurred here, most of them sailing vessels. The coast's north-setting current accelerated dramatically in bad weather, often causing ships to underestimate their positions. It was always difficult to navigate around Cape Flattery and find the narrow neck of Juan de Fuca Strait, but when winter clouds and summer fogs prevented celestial observation, ships could easily lose their bearings, miss the critical turn east, and be swept north by the current onto the rocky coast ahead.

The first lighthouse on the West Coast was built in 1873 at Cape Beale, the promontory at the southern entrance to Barkley Sound, a lonely, isolated location. At first its only way of communicating with Victoria was by rowboat; an Indian brought the mail by dugout canoe for five dollars, a six-day round-trip journey of 180 miles. Light-keepers could not call for help for ships in distress, or for themselves if sickness or broken machinery required it. Then in 1890, the government started construction of a telegraph line, a single wire strung between trees along the coast from

Left — *Waves dashing the rocks at Port Renfrew, west coast of Vancouver Island, illustrate the power and savagery of the ocean here in the Graveyard of the Pacific. The strong northerly currents along the coast swept vessels along far more quickly than they estimated, causing errors in location. Hidden reefs and rocks and sudden, fierce storms dashed many ships to their deaths.* (Bill Staley)
Right — *Evidence of the many shipwrecks can still be seen along the coast. This is what remains of the* Vanlene *in Pacific Rim National Park, west coast of Vancouver Island.* (B.C. Parks)

Lighthouses such as this one on Race Rocks, at the southern tip of Vancouver Island, gave ships their positions and steered them away from dangerous reefs. Race Rocks today are an ecological reserve set up to preserve the sea lion population. (B.C. Government)

Victoria to Cape Beale. It was at best a frail, sporadic lifeline: a single tree falling across it in a storm would put it out of action. To maintain the line, each twenty-five-mile section was patrolled on foot by a lineman, along a primitive trail.

In 1906, the steamer *Valencia* left San Francisco for Victoria and Vancouver with 164 passengers and crew. Lost in a howling gale at dead of night, she holed on a rock, took on water fast, and desperately drove toward land. But she lodged on a reef some thirty yards out from the cliffs of Pachena Point, south of Cape Beale. Lifeboats were lowered, but the breakers overturned them, washing the occupants into the sea. Four lifeboats were lost; the electric power on the ship failed and the captain decided to wait on board for daylight. More boats were then launched and some men managed to reach the shore, find their way to the skimpy trail under the wireless line and head to the lighthouse for help. Several passing ships stopped to give aid to the stricken vessel but the waves were too high for them to get near; all they could do was watch as the *Valencia* broke into pieces on the rocks and the men and women on board were dashed into the surf. There were only 38 survivors; and of the rest, only 59 bodies were ever recovered.

This shipwreck horrified British Columbians and an official enquiry was launched. Eleven months later, when once again the telegraph line was disabled by a storm, the ship *Coloma* was wrecked on the rocks below Cape Beale lighthouse. This time, passengers and crew were saved because the lighthouse keeper's wife ran five miles through the bush to Bamfield to summon help from the government ship *Quadra*. (Ironically, Bamfield did have a reliable telegraph service — to Australia by way of the Pacific submarine cable, completed in 1902.)

This second shipwreck brought action more useful than an enquiry. Lifesaving stations were immediately planned at Clo-oose, Bamfield and Ucluelet, a new lighthouse was constructed at Pachena Point, and thirty miles of lifesaving trail were built along the notorious stretch of coast. A string of tiny cabins stocked with blankets and provisions provided shelter for survivors along the trail. Scores of shipwrecked mariners who made it to shore owe their lives to these little cabins and the trail that led to civilization.

Modern rescue methods and better communications ultimately made the trail obsolete, but today this section of coastline is part of Pacific Rim National Park and the restored trail is being walked again, this time by recreational hikers who enjoy the wilderness forests and wave-dashed coastline of this beautiful and treacherous coastline.

Exploring the Wrecks

Searching for and exploring the old shipwrecks has become a popular pursuit for SCUBA divers. Some of the wrecks washed up onto the shore and are now well-known landmarks. Some sank to the sea bottom in water so deep they may never be found, but most came to rest on the shallow continental shelf. Here they lie, time capsules of the eighteenth and nineteenth centuries, waiting to be found. While there is little likelihood of Spanish or Cariboo gold lying in waterlogged hulls, there is treasure of another kind: artifacts and memorabilia that can fetch high prices from collectors.

B.C. has an active Underwater Archeological Society whose members have found and "excavated" the remains of several important shipwrecks, including the *Robert Kerr*. Built in 1866 as a sailing ship, later

Lighthouse at Amphitrite Point, west coast of Vancouver Island.
(Fisheries Council of B.C.)

Sunset over English Bay, Vancouver, is punctuated by the tiny blinking light of Point Atkinson Lighthouse, West Vancouver, which guards the entrance to the outer harbour.
(Bill Staley)

134

Above left — *Chrome Island Lighthouse supplies are brought in by helicopter.* (B.C. Government)
Above — *The West Coast Trail from Bamfield to Port Renfrew was originally known as the Lifesaving Trail because it provided a route for shipwrecked mariners through the forest. The trail is rugged, with ladders needed in places.* (B.C. Parks)
Left — *Hikers walk a section of beach along the West Coast Trail, a fifty-mile hike which takes about five days.* (Greg Maurer — Photo/Graphics)

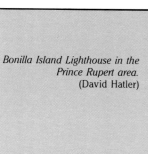

Bonilla Island Lighthouse in the Prince Rupert area.
(David Hatler)

converted to a coal barge, she sank in 1911 in the Gulf Islands. The *Robert Kerr* played a part in Vancouver's great moments of history. On April 6, 1886, the three-masted barque was in Vancouver harbour helping the new city celebrate its incorporation. And two months later, anchored off Hastings Mill, she became a refuge for two hundred survivors of the Great Fire which levelled the city.

Another ship excavated by the society is the U.S. ship *Ericsson,* which foundered in 1892 in Barkley Sound and which was discovered, still beautifully intact, in 1985. This ship, considered by the Vancouver Maritime Museum to be one of the most important wrecks ever found in B.C., was originally fitted with revolutionary caloric engines which ran on hot air instead of steam. These proved a failure, so the boat was refitted with steam engines and then, curiously, her engines were removed and she reverted to sail.

The prize catch for the underwater archeologists, if they could find it, would be the American fur-trading ship *Tonquin,* which sank in 1811 somewhere off Clayuquot Sound after Indian troubles. The ship's captain had insulted the local Indian chief, and to avenge him the tribesmen seized the ship and her contents and massacred most of the crew. One crew-member, however, was able to get below decks and he tossed a lighted taper into the ship's supplies of gunpowder. The explosion killed him and about two hundred Indians and took the *Tonquin* to a watery

The West Coast Trail passes mostly through dense forest with ladders for access. It is now part of Pacific Rim National Park.
(David Hatler)

grave. So far this historic ship, by now likely buried under tons of sand and sediment, has eluded discovery, despite sophisticated electronic location techniques.

Hiking the West Coast Trail

First merely a path through the woods for telephone linemen, then an access route for shipwrecked mariners, the West Coast Trail today is one of the most popular wilderness hikes in British Columbia. Preserved within a section of Pacific Rim National Park, the trail is neither short nor easy. With full backpacks, it requires a minimum of five days of strenuous hiking. There are no facilities except for wilderness campsites along the trail; no stores, no accommodations, no roads, no emergency help.

The trail traverses some fifty miles of wild, mostly uninhabited shoreline between Port Renfrew and Bamfield on the west coast of Vancouver Island, a coastline battered by fierce storms and deluged by almost constant rains. The terrain is rugged: the steep, rocky shoreline is gashed by inlets and roaring rivers and to navigate them the trail needs suspension bridges, five cable crossings, two boat crossings, numerous ladders and stretches of boardwalk. The forests are thick and dank, the mosquitoes lively, the weather usually terrible. Yet each year the trail lures an increasing number of hardy hikers.

The trail's appeal is easy to understand: at the raw edge of a continent, it offers wild, wave-dashed headlands and long stretches of empty sand; rock ledges and tidepools, the sounds and smells of the ocean and the forest, a chance for solitude. Trail highlights include the sea caves at Tsuquadra and Tsusiat Point; Tsusiat Falls, which tumbles over a sixty-foot cliff right into the ocean, a favorite camping spot; Nitinat Narrows, the constricted mouth of a long tidal lake where the tide roars through at eight knots, which must be crossed in an Indian boat; lighthouses at Carmanah and Pachena points; a sea-lion rookery and Indian villages at Clo-ose and Whyac.

To reach the southern trailhead, hikers must drive logging roads from Victoria or Cowichan Lake. Bamfield at the northern end is reached by logging road or boat from Port Alberni. The *Lady Rose* makes return trips down Alberni Inlet to Bamfield three times a week, with extra Sunday trips in summer.

Right — *Waterfall at the south end of the trail near Port Renfrew.* (David Hatler)

Resources Today

Fishing

The North Pacific Ocean is nutritionally one of the richest seas on earth and in the past it has supported huge numbers of salmon, herring, halibut and many other species of fish. The most important commercial fish is salmon. Stocks dwindled sharply in the first thirty years of the twentieth century due to drastic overfishing, but since 1937, Canadian and international laws have monitored and regulated all five species — sockeye, coho, chum, chinook and pink — and today the stocks are said to be recovering. Salmonid enhancement programs, which consist of improving the spawning ground in coastal rivers, fertilizing lakes where the young fish live during the first years of their lives, and raising fish in hatcheries, are assisting in this recovery. B.C. fishermen netted some 98,000 tons of salmon in 1985, up from the yearly average of 63,000 tons, but much of this increase is thought to be due to the overlapping of peak four-year cycles within the different races. B.C. salmon accounts for twelve percent of the world catch, and it is marketed canned, frozen, fresh and smoked. Half of the canned salmon and eighty percent of the frozen are exported, mostly to Europe.

Herring is the second most valuable commercial species

Left — *Off Prince Rupert, troll-caught salmon gets a hearty heave.* (Fisheries Council of B.C.)
Right — *Sunset at Coal Harbour, once a whaling station at the east end of Quatsino Sound; a troller displays its catch of salmon ready dressed for the freezer.* (Fisheries Council of B.C.)

Offloading a catch of pink and sockeye salmon for grading.
(Fisheries Council of B.C.)

and one equally devastated by overfishing. Herring is caught principally for its roe, which is marketed in Japan (the rest of the fish is rendered for fertilizer), but today this fishery is in a strong conservation mode; it is banned completely in southern waters (south of the northern tip of Vancouver Island) at least through 1986 to give stocks a chance to recover. Herring quotas are thus reduced from an annual average of 30,000 tons to 12,000 tons.

A more encouraging picture emerges for halibut, the third most important fishery. Under the jurisdiction of the International Halibut Commission, stocks of this fish are increasing and are expected to stabilize at close to sustainable yield levels. Most of the 5,000-ton halibut catch is exported to the United States and Japan. Other ground fish such as cod, sole and snapper and several kinds of shellfish, including crab and clams, are also fished commercially.

The B.C. fishing industry currently accounts for about 12,000 direct and 25,000 indirect jobs in British Columbia, with the industry centred still in traditional fishing grounds around the mouth of the Fraser River in the south and the Skeena River in the north. There are today, however, only a dozen fish processing plants, one of them, Ocean Fisheries, Ltd. in Richmond, which opened in 1985, said to be the most modern in the world.

Some people predict that the future of B.C.'s food production from the sea lies increasingly with mariculture or fish farming. The B.C. Coast with its many bays and inlets is ideal for such an industry. Oysters have been grown commercially here for many years, but until recently the spat (fertilized oyster seed) had to be imported because local waters are generally too cold for natural spawning. Today, however, shellfish hatcheries in a few ideal locations are providing grown-in-B.C. oyster spat. Traditional oyster farms are located in shallow waters along protected beaches, but this combination is hard to find along B.C.'s rocky coast, and so here, oysters are grown hanging from floats in deep water. These "off-bottom" oysters grow whiter, larger and faster than beach oysters.

Abalone are also being raised artificially, using submerged black plastic plates, though at present more for seed

Below — *The Indians of the coast were always skillful fishermen and many, such as this Haida, still practise the craft.* (Jurgen Vogt — Photo/Graphics)

Above — *Fish are offloaded in huge plastic tubs and hauled by crane onto the dock.* (Fisheries Council of B.C.)

A purse seine, its net set in the distinctive circle.
(Fisheries Council of B.C.)

A gillnetter hauls in his catch. (Fisheries Council of B.C.)

Its net stowed, its catch freezing in the hold, a fishboat and its crew take a momentary rest. (Fisheries Council of B.C.)

Right — *Fishing fleet, Prince Rupert Harbour.* (Fisheries Council of B.C.)

Above — *B.C. coastal waters abound in many varieties of shellfish. Crabs are particularly plentiful.*
(David Hatler)
Top right — *Crab fisherman hauls in his trap.*
(David Hatler)
Right — *Aerial view of an oyster farm. Oyster spat is grown on huge rafts floating in deep water.*
(Lyn Hancock)

Top — *West Coast troller.* (Fisheries Council of B.C.)
Above — *Gillnetter at the mouth of the Skeena River.* (Fisheries Council of B.C.)

Top — *Fish packer.* (Fisheries Council of B.C.)
Above — *Fish boats rest in harbour near Port Hardy, Vancouver Island.* (Gunter Marx — Photo/Graphics)

production in wild abalone beds than for commercial use. Wild abalone are slow growers, taking up to ten years to reach the legal four-inch size. Cultured abalone could be brought to market far earlier. Even chinook and coho salmon are being spawned and raised along the coast, first in freshwater tanks to simulate a river environment, then in net-enclosed pens suspended in sheltered bays. Experiments are also underway for the commercial farming of scallops, clams and mussels, primarily at the fishing village of Bamfield on Vancouver Island's west coast.

The Forests

The forests are B.C.'s single greatest resource, yet at first they were considered of no special worth. Covering the land so thickly and growing so tall, they seemed to impede the progress of settlement and road-building, and the first governments were anxious to have as much as possible cut and cleared.

The building of the Canadian Pacific Railway, the link that joined the new confederation of Canada from east to west in 1885, opened prairie and coastal lands for immigration. A land rush hit the provinces of Alberta, Saskatchewan and Manitoba around the turn of the century, and as new settlements mushroomed, so did the demand for B.C. lumber, which could easily be shipped east along the new rails.

At about the same time, American lumbermen in the east began to run out of trees. They naturally looked to the Northwest for more, and to Canada in particular because of laxer restrictions. In B.C., exclusive cutting rights to one square mile of forest could be claimed by anyone who drove in a corner post and paid a nominal rent. The Americans were also the first to realize that northwest lumber would be worth more as soon as the Panama Canal was finished and shipment to Europe made more economical. In 1910, investment in the B.C. forest industry amounted to around $2 million, all of it Canadian. Ten years later, investment had grown to $65 million, 90 percent of it American. With this infusion of American know-how and capital, the forest

Left — *Morning mist shrouds the shore at the fishing community of Steveston at the mouth of the Fraser.* (Gunter Marx — Photo/Graphics)
Above — *Chain saw slices through a tall red cedar. The original forests of cedar and Douglas fir have nearly all been logged and second-growth trees are not given time to grow to full size before being logged again.* (Bob Herger — Photo/Graphics)
Right — *So tall it seems to curve toward the sky, this cedar will soon be toppled.* (Council of Forest Industries)

Above — *Logging roads take the industry up onto high plateaus and mountain slopes. Patches of clear-cutting checkerboard the nearby ridge. Vancouver Island.* (Council of Forest Industries)

Right — *Logs are hauled by truck along many miles of logging roads, making even distant forests accessible to the industry.* (Council of Forest Industry)

152

Log-booming with a dozer-boat, eastern Vancouver Island. Log booms are hauled by barge along the coast to centrally located mills. (Council of Forest Industries)

industry boomed. Logging railways plunged ever deeper into the coastal mountains; mills and mill towns sprang up like weeds. The virgin forests toppled.

The first timber lands to be cut were the best: the dense forests of Douglas fir easily accessible by tidewater along the southern sheltered coasts and on Vancouver Island. After 1896, forested land in the province was leased, not sold outright. Thus, today the people of B.C. still own ninety-three percent of the province's forests. Of the remaining seven percent, some was sold, some given away as incentives for railway builders. The original land grant of the Esquimalt and Nanaimo Railway, for example was for three thousand square miles!

In that logging boom era, everyone believed that cut forests would soon grow again, regenerating themselves naturally. Quick and careless logging practices left the denuded land in appalling condition, with stumps six and eight feet high surrounded by a sad litter of wasted timber. In 1912 the B.C. government started to clamp down on forest waste. Timber owners were made to contribute to a forest protection fund and, more important, pay stumpage rates based on the assessed amount of timber on the lease, rather than on the amount actually cut. In 1945 the B.C. government officially adopted a sustained yield policy of forest management, but this, even if it had been acted on in light of today's knowledge of silviculture, was already too late.

Clear-cutting was (and still is) a common industry practice, one that most other countries consider too harmful to be permitted. Many of B.C.'s steep mountain slopes, stripped of trees, their soil incinerated by uncontrolled slash burning, fall easy prey to water erosion. In these areas of thin soil, exposed bedrock and cold, incessant rain, forests of

Top left — *Scaling logs. The trees cut today are far smaller than B.C. trees used to be.* (Council of Forest Industries)

Above — *Clear-cutting and erosion from logging roads leave their scars on the forested mountain slopes. This is eastern Vancouver Island near Nanaimo.* (Lyn Hancock)

Left — *Giant machines are used to load and offload the logs onto trailers as the industry becomes increasingly mechanized.* (Council of Forest Industries)

Anthony Island Provincial Park

Remaining totems of the deserted village of Ninstints on Anthony Island. Many were taken to mainland museums. (B.C. Parks)

When Captain George Dixon anchored his ship, the *Queen Charlotte,* off the southernmost tip of a remote chain of North Pacific islands in July, 1787, eleven large canoes laden with one hundred eighty people came to greet him. They were inhabitants of Ninstints, the main village of the Kunghit Haida, who occupied all of the southern Queen Charlotte Islands from Lyell Island south. Dixon found the village large and prosperous, with a population of between three and four hundred. There were many large ceremonial houses and a veritable forest of carved totem poles lining the shore. He also found the Haida eager to trade pelts of the sea otter for white man's goods. For the next forty years, until the extermination of the otter, Ninstints on the eastern shore of tiny Anthony Island was one of the most important trading centres on the Pacific Coast.

At the time of white contact, the Kunghit Haida had about two dozen large, permanent villages throughout their territory and their society was thriving. In 1862, a devastating epidemic of smallpox hit the coast. Whole villages succumbed to the disease and the Kunghit Haida in particular were decimated. In 1886, the thirty remaining inhabitants of Ninsints, the largest

Left — *Anthony Island totems, still noble in decay.* (Edward Gifford — Photo/Graphics)
Above — *The totems of Anthony Island have been shored up to prevent further decay in this world heritage site.* (B.C. Parks)

village, moved north to join other survivors at Skidegate. The village was deserted, its decorated houses and the long array of house, mortuary and memorial poles abandoned to time and the elements, a hundred years of rain and rot and rampant forest growth. For eighty years, it was left in solitude.

In the 1950s, interest in the site was rekindled. Some of the poles were removed to the mainland for preservation in museums. In 1958 the village site was made a provincial park. The offshore islets and shores of Anthony Island were declared a provincial ecological reserve in 1979, and the following year the whole island was designated a provincial archeological and heritage site. In 1981 the village was declared a UNESCO World Heritage Site, and preservation began. The encroaching spruce forest has been cut back and all existing poles have been carefully cleared of growing tufts of fern and salal, tree seedlings and roots, thick moss and lichens. Poles in danger of total collapse have been shored up, but those already fallen have been left to rejoin the earth, as fallen poles were meant to do in the days of Haida occupation.

Because of its isolated position, Anthony Island does not yet receive many visitors. Access is, in any case, restricted. Visitors must have written permission from the B.C. Parks and Recreation Division in Victoria before they can land. In the summer months a Haida caretaker keeps watch over the village, living in a traditional style longhouse prefabricated in Terrace and shipped to the island.

Despite the best efforts of the conservationists, the Haida village of Ninstints and the creatures — bear, frog, whale, eagle and raven — that decorate its monumental architecture will ultimately decay. Meanwhile it is one of the most impressive of the Coast Indian sites, one most definitely worth a visit.

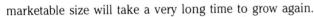

marketable size will take a very long time to grow again.

The 1940s also saw some initial efforts at tree-planting, a procedure that if done conscientiously and consistently might ensure a continuous supply of mature trees. But the amount of replanting done then and even today is dishearteningly low. The 75 million trees planted annually are enough to restock only about one-third of the logged acreage. Forestry malpractice has been going on for so long in B.C. that a serious shortfall is soon anticipated. Even the most optimistic now agree that the province will run out of old forests in about ten years, and that more of the less productive second-growth forests will need to be cut to keep supplies constant. These second-growth forests are not growing so fast nor so well as predicted. Shortages of Douglas fir and cedar are considered the most serious.

In 1985, moves by the federal and provincial governments and even the forest unions to increase reforestation seemed promising. But 1985 was also one of the worst years on record for forest fires: about 600,000 acres burned during the dry summer. The cost of fighting the fires amounted to more than $123 million, but the loss to the B.C. forest industry at this critical time is incalculable.

Left — *Log booms, Cowichan Lake.* (B.C. Government)
Top — *There are not many tall trees left but a chain saw soon cuts them down to size.* (Council of Forest Industries)
Above — *Log patrol vessel* Shadow *polices Howe Sound on the lookout for log poachers. In the distance, the white plume of the pulp mill at Woodfibre.* (Council of Forest Industries)

*Sawmill and booming grounds, Campbell River
estuary, Vancouver Island.* (B.C. Government)

Mineral Resources

Very little mining is carried out west of the Coast Mountain divide, though B.C. is Canada's largest exporter of copper, molybdenum and coal and much is shipped from coastal ports. Huge specialized coal-handling facilities have been built at the bulk terminals of Roberts Bank, south of Vancouver, and Ridley Island, near Prince Rupert, for the major market is Japan. Likewise there are few known oil or natural gas deposits in coastal B.C., though investigations are underway for shale oil in the Queen Charlottes and for natural gas on Vancouver Island. Studies are also being done to evaluate the effects of drilling for offshore oil on the continental shelf north of Vancouver Island, though problems of ownership and jurisdiction have yet to be resolved.

The B.C. Coast is already in much jeopardy from the transshipment of oil. More than 800,000 barrels are transported annually from Alaska to Washington and California along a coast notorious for its bad weather and navigation hazards. Already it is estimated that nearly half a million sea birds die every year from oil pollution; 2.5 million tons of oil are lost annually in the world's oceans, most in the northern hemisphere. A supertanker spill or wreck off the coast could bring disaster to birds and marine life, and could directly affect the whole intertwined ecosystem on which man is dependent.

Recreation and Tourism

Perhaps the greatest resource of the British Columbia coast is its capacity for recreation and tourism. The thousands of miles of shoreline, though in places badly scarred by clear-cut logging, still provide a beauty and a wilderness quality eagerly sought in a world increasingly urbanized. The coast cities themselves draw tourists — Vancouver because it is Canada's third largest, a laid-back cosmopolitan metropolis; Victoria because of its cosy "English" charm — but most come to enjoy the beauty of the maritime and mountain scenery.

It is prime country for outdoorsmen, particularly those

Above — *Iron-ore mine tailings dwarf the townsite at Tasu, west coast Queen Charlotte Islands. Mine opened in 1965 and produced a million tons of iron and copper concentrate annually. The company town housed 350 people. Today, the mine closed, the town is virtually a ghost.* (David Hatler)
Right/left — *In contrast to a landscape scarred by mining and logging, B.C.'s provincial parks show nature at its untouched best. Hikers enjoy this view of Garibaldi Lake from the alpine meadows of Panorama Ridge.* (Abson — Photo/Graphics)

Left — *Recreation and tourism are important factors in the B.C. economy. The M.V.* Lady Rose *takes passengers and cargo down Alberni Inlet to the west coast of Vancouver Island, stopping in the Broken Islands to offload canoeists.* (Lyn Hancock)

Right — *There are three mountains directly north of Vancouver that have been developed for skiing. The views of the city from Grouse, Seymour and Cypress Bowl are stunning.* (Jurgen Vogt — Photo/Graphics)

Above — *A float plane and canoes, Darcy Island. The coast is explored in all sorts of ways.* (Lyn Hancock)

Above centre — *Vancouver's many parks are enjoyed year-round. This is Lost Lagoon in Stanley Park, after a fresh snowfall.* (Phil Hersee)

Above right — *The popularity of recreational boating has reached almost epidemic proportions along the south coast. Aerial view over Indian Arm northeast of Vancouver shows the water streaked with pleasure craft.* (Bill Staley)

interested in wildlife and native Indian culture. Several ferries and cruise ships and thousands of small pleasure boats ply the scenic Inside Passage and the mazy waterways between the Gulf Islands. Sports fishing, sailing, canoeing, scuba diving, hiking, cycling, camping, mountain-climbing, auto-touring, are all popular pursuits for residents and tourists alike. And while some accessible areas are beginning to experience overcrowding in the peak summer season, there are others where loneliness is pretty much guaranteed.

The coast is well endowed with parks. The largest are mountain reserves: Tweedsmuir, nearly 2.5 million acres, east of Bella Coola; Strathcona, 600,000 acres in the centre of Vancouver Island, and Garibaldi, 480,000 acres, northeast of Howe Sound. Naikoon Provincial Park, 180,000 acres,

includes lowland forest and long, sandy beaches at the north-eastern edge of Graham Island. Pacific Rim National Park on the west coast of Vancouver Island is in three separate locations: the shoreline between Tofino and Ucluelet; the Broken Islands in the mouth of Barkley Sound, and a narrow strip of shore traversed by the historic West Coast Trail between Port Renfrew and Bamfield. Cape Scott, 62,000 acres, is a wilderness park at the northwestern tip of Vancouver Island.

Most of the other parks along the coast are small marine enclaves, not accessible by road and intended primarily for the use of recreational boaters. There are twenty-eight of these marine parks, and there are others that have no road access, such as Anthony Island, an abandoned Haida Indian

Sailing is popular all year, especially in English Bay and Howe Sound, even when mountaintops are white with fresh snow. (Gunter Marx — Photo/Graphics)

village in the southwest Queen Charlottes, designated a world heritage site, and the rock on which explorer Alexander Mackenzie commemorated his arrival "from Canada, by land" in 1793. Largest of the marine parks is Desolation Sound, with more than forty miles of shoreline and several offshore islands. The waters of the sound are among the warmest on the coast, ideal for scuba diving.

Several new provincial parks have been proposed for the coast. These include Hunter and Calvert islands, both near Rivers Inlet, and both relatively unlogged tracts of coast lowland forest; and Mussel Inlet, a classic example of a fjord landscape. The South Moresby area of the Queen Charlottes has been recommended for national park status. The islands' wilderness mountains and teeming shores support many rare and a few unique species of wildlife in addition to a rich Indian history.

The province also has more than one hundred ecological reserves. B.C. was the first Canadian province to set aside natural areas for total protection, refuges for plants and animals where man is allowed only as an observer. Representative samples of the great diversity of different environments found in the province, these reserves include bogs and marshes, desert, forest, alpine meadows, lakes, hot springs, islands, grasslands — all living museums of sometimes very fragile ecosystems. Some of these are as small as an acre; some stretch to 120,000 acres. There are thirty reserves along the coast and fifteen of these are islands set aside to protect nesting colonies of sea birds and marine wildlife, including the sea-lion rookeries and haul-outs at Race Rocks at the southern tip of Vancouver Island and the Kerouard Islands of the southern Queen Charlottes. Others protect virgin or well-preserved stands of coastal forest, subtidal marine life, rare flowers and ferns (the white avalanche lily on San Juan Ridge, the adder's tongue fern at Sutton's Pass, both Vancouver Island), or unique fish (the stickleback of Drizzle Lake in the Queen Charlottes). Two were established in the Charlottes to protect sand dunes, another to preserve a beach in Johnstone Strait where killer whales congregate.

165

Canada's Inside Passage

One of the many cruise ships that ply the Strait of Georgia crosses the mouth of Howe Sound. (Rick Marotz — Photo/Graphics)

Along the inner coast of British Columbia, most of it fully protected from the open ocean, the Inside Passage threads its way north through a maze of islands and inlets from the Washington border to Alaska. Giant tankers and tugboats, barges and fish boats, luxury liners and sailing vessels and small family cruisers all ply these waters, some of the most scenic in the world. Alaska ferries sail this route all the way from Seattle but B.C. ferries cruise only the northern section, from Port Hardy on Vancouver Island.

The Alaska ferry route heads north up the Strait of Georgia, passing to the west of Texada and Lasqueti islands, then squeezing through narrow Discovery Passage between Vancouver and Quadra islands. At the tightest section, Seymour Narrows still requires tricky sailing for the tide streams through at up to fifteen knots. This was the site of infamous Ripple Rock, an underwater obstruction that was blasted out of existence in 1958 in the largest manmade non-nuclear explosion in the world. Discovery Passage was named for Captain Vancouver's ship; Quadra Island, for the Spanish explorer and commander of the fort at Nootka. Sonora Island, separated by only a slim strait from Quadra Island, and named after Quadra's ship, lies off the mouth of Bute Inlet. At the time of the Cariboo gold rush, promoter Alfred Waddington started to build a road from the head of this inlet up the Homathco River as a shortcut to the gold fields. The road crew was massacred by Indians and the project was abandoned.

The ferry rounds the corner of Vancouver Island at Chatham Point, named for the small armed tender that accompanied Vancouver's *Discovery,* and heads into Johnstone Strait. The mainland to the north is fractured into a puzzle of islands and long inlets, among the latter Loughborough and Knight. Near the head of Knight Inlet lies Mount Waddington, second highest peak in B.C. In contrast to the mainland, the Vancouver Island shore is almost unbroken except for several small indentations. Half way through the strait, one of these indentations is Kelsey Bay, a former B.C. Ferry terminal. Farther north is the mouth of the Tsitika River at Robson Bight, site of a provincial ecological reserve set aside to protect the orca, or killer whales, which congregate here. This is said to be the best place in the world to see orcas. The next small notch is the harbour of Beaver Cove, site of former HBC Fort Rupert and the small community of Telegraph Cove. Opposite are tiny Cormorant Island and the community of Alert Bay, reached by small ferry from Port McNeill. Alert Bay is a vital Indian community; its totem poles, one of them the world's largest, should be visible from the ferry.

The busy fishing harbour of Port McNeill is opposite larger Malcolm Island, site of a former Finnish community and its settlement, Sointula. Port Hardy, a few miles farther north along the Vancouver Island coast, is the start point for the B.C. Ferry Service. From Port Hardy the ferries go out into Queen

Charlotte Strait, the only unprotected stretch of ocean in the entire voyage and hazardous to small boats in rough weather. Once around Cape Caution, the ferries quickly duck into Fitz Hugh Sound behind the shelter of Calvert Island. To the north lies the mouth of Rivers Inlet, once almost lined with fish canneries. Today it is famous for sports fishing and there are several fly-in resorts along its shores, at least one in a converted historic cannery.

Onward the ferries steam, past the mouth of Burke Channel (Bella Coola lies at its head) and through Lama Passage to Bella Bella, a fishing village once the site of HBC Fort McLaughlin. A B.C. ferry calls in here once a week with passengers and supplies. On Campbell Island opposite the village is the Indian settlement of Waglisla. To the east lies Dean Channel,

Logging equipment is towed by barge up Grenville Channel, one of the narrowest and straightest of B.C.'s fjords. (Jurgen Vogt — Photo/Graphics)

The B.C. Coast is fractured into a maze of islands, making for tricky navigation, but splendid maritime scenery. (Herger-Burridge — Photo/Graphics)

salt water emetics. Mussel Inlet, a classic fjord, has been proposed as a new provincial park. Other park proposals are for relatively unlogged Calvert and Hunter islands, to the south.

To the west of Finlayson Channel lies Swindle Island; on its western peninsula is one of the very few volcanic cones on the coast, a little hill eight hundred feet high. At the north end of the island the ferries leave comparatively roomy Finlayson Channel and enter the narrow passage east of Princess Royal Island. Princess Royal Channel and the island behind, which it hides, were named not for royalty but for the ship of fur-trader Captain Charles Duncan in 1788.

Out of the narrow confines of the channel and across the wide mouth of Douglas Channel (Kitimat lies at its head) the ferries next plunge into the long, skinny and very straight Grenville Channel sheltered behind Pitt Island. Across the mouth of the Skeena River and into Chatham Sound, the B.C. ferry reaches its destination of Prince Rupert on Kaien Island, the Indian name for the froth which is beaten up by strong rapids at the island's southern end after heavy rains.

Prince Rupert was founded by a United States citizen, Charles Hayes, who was the first to see its potential as a world port and to lobby for its choice as terminal of a transcontinental railway. He bought Kaien Island from the natives and founded a town. Hayes lived to see the railway arrive in 1908, but four years later he was drowned on the *Titanic* and the impetus for development was lost. Today, however, the thriving port city vindicates his vision.

Alaska ferries continue north along the Inside Passage for another four days, all the way to Skagway. B.C. ferries connect at Prince Rupert for the Queen Charlotte Islands, sixty miles offshore.

made famous by explorer Alexander Mackenzie, who painted his name and the date on a rock here to prove that he had made his epic overland voyage to the Pacific Ocean. A small provincial park, reached only by boat, now marks the spot.

From Bella Bella the voyage continues into Seaforth Channel, around Lady Douglas Island, named for the wife of B.C.'s first governor, and into Finlayson Channel, the deepest waters of all the fjords along the coast. At the head of Mathieson Channel to the east lies Mussel Inlet, and at its head is Poison Cove. These names commemorate a nasty incident that took place here during Captain Vancouver's coastal exploration. A seaman, John Carter, died from eating toxic mussels and was buried at nearby Carter Bay. The rest of the crew escaped death by drinking hot

Infamous Ripple Rock

The world's greatest peacetime, non-nuclear, manmade explosion took place in April, 1958, in Discovery Passage between Vancouver and Maud islands. The explosion, which used nearly 1,300 tons of TNT, removed one of the Pacific Coast's worst marine hazards — Ripple Rock, an underwater miniature mountain block 120 by 170 feet, with two main peaks and eleven separate pinnacles which reached to within ten feet of the water surface.

The neck of tight Discovery Passage is Seymour Narrows, only eight hundred yards wide, where the tidal current often roars through at greater than twelve knots, creating dangerous currents and whirlpools. Ripple Rock was right in the middle of this tight and hazardous channel. Since the U.S. naval steamship *Saranac* was dashed to death here in 1875, the rock has sunk or crippled more than a hundred ships and claimed one hundred twenty lives.

Ripple Rock was an acknowledged hazard in the international sealanes, but several previous attempts to destroy it were foiled by the turbulence of the waters. On the first try, cables anchoring the drilling barge were snapped by strong currents. On a second, the drilling barge was successfully anchored by overhead cables but a boat carrying nine men to work on the drills capsized in the currents and all the men were drowned.

Instead of trying to drill down from the water surface, the third attempt tunnelled under the water from Maud Island and planted explosives in the base of the rock, a laborious process that took two and a half years to complete at a cost of more than $3 million. But it was successful. The explosion, detonated on a spring day in 1958, blew rock and water ten thousand feet into the air, and reduced the mountain of Ripple Rock to a mere underwater hump more than forty feet below the low-water line.

Seymour Narrows today is rid of its greatest hazard, but it still requires skillful navigation; the tides in this narrow end of the funnel are still fierce and the waters turbulent. Even a small error here could spell disaster. In June of 1984, the cruise ship *Sundancer*, bound for Alaska along B.C.'s scenic Inside Passage, was hurled onto the rocks of Maud Island and ripped apart. Her crew and eight hundred passengers were saved, but Seymour Narrows had claimed yet another victim.

Ripple Rock was blasted out of existence in 1958 to clear the passage for safe shipping. The explosion used 1,300 tons of TNT, cost $3 million. (B.C. Archives)

Coast Communities

The city of Vancouver, spread out between Burrard Inlet to the north and the Fraser River to the south, is the third largest metropolitan area in Canada, housing nearly 1.5 million people — nearly half the population of British Columbia. It is the province's economic heart, the centre of manufacturing, trade and commerce, one of North America's busiest ports (the leading dry-cargo port on the Pacific), home base for a large commercial fishing fleet, and the home of B.C.'s two largest universities, University of B.C. and Simon Fraser. Linked by railways and roads to Washington State, the B.C. interior and the rest of Canada, by ferry system and cruise ship to Vancouver Island, Prince Rupert and Alaska, and by air to the rest of the world, Vancouver is also B.C.'s single largest tourist destination.

The city's magnificent mountain and maritime setting, its benign climate and cosmopolitan atmosphere account for its popularity. It has a full complement of museums, art galleries, shops, restaurants, sports complexes (including a new dome stadium) and other urban attributes. And just as important, the forested trails of thousand-acre Stanley Park, downtown, and the mountains of the North Shore provide an additional element — of accessible wilderness — that heightens the urban experience.

Left — *New condominium complexes have recently replaced industry on the south shore of False Creek. Across Granville and Burrard bridges at the inlet mouth lie the highrises of Vancouver's West End.* (B.C. Government)
Right — *Lions Gate suspension bridge links Vancouver to the communities of North and West Vancouver.* (Bill Staley)

Above — *Robson Square in the heart of downtown Vancouver. The old courthouse (centre) has been converted into an art gallery. The steep green roof (copper sheathing) is the Hotel Vancouver.* (Phil Hersee)
Right — *Vancouver is a city deeply fingered by the sea. False Creek is a popular moorage for pleasure boats.* (Vancouver Visitors Bureau)
Far right — *New development on Granville Island, at the south end of Granville bridge, includes a popular public market, biking and jogging trails and this children's area.* (Bill Staley)

174

A distinctive feature of the city is its diverse ethnic makeup. Vancouver's Chinatown is the second largest in North America; only San Francisco's is larger. Chinatown is not an ethnic ghetto. Sandwiched between the old part of the city (Gastown) and the False Creek site of the 1986 World Exposition, it is today one of Vancouver's most dynamic inner-city neighborhoods, complete with fashionable housing, a large new Cultural Centre with the only full-scale classical Chinese garden in North America, and Chinese language newspapers. Tourists and residents take pleasure in its exotic atmosphere, its streets of Chinese greengrocers, fishmongers, poulterers and herbalists, its scores of restaurants and gift shops. Its New Year and other celebrations bring excitement to Vancouver streets.

Other large and colorful ethnic communities include Italian, Japanese, East Indian and Greek, all with their own shopping areas, churches and ethnic events.

B.C.'s capital city, Victoria is far smaller than Vancouver. With a population of around 65,000 (area, 220,000), its economic mainstay is the government, with tourism not far behind. On the southwestern tip of Vancouver Island, Victoria enjoys B.C.'s most salubrious climate and a cosy English atmosphere retained from its long history as a Hudson's Bay fort and outpost of the British Empire. It and satellite communities on the Saanich Peninsula are favorite retirement centres for Canadians from other provinces, who willingly exchange their long, severe winters for Victoria's roses in December. Sometimes, however, coast winters play tricks. In 1985, for instance, November was one of the coldest and snowiest on record, and unusual outflow wind conditions resulted in balmy Victoria's receiving far more cold and snow than the mainland.

Victoria is linked by ferries to Vancouver (by way of the Canadian Gulf Islands), Seattle and Anacortes, Washington (by way of the San Juan Islands).

Between Vancouver Island and the mainland, lying like stepping stones in the sheltered Strait of Georgia, the Gulf Islands are known for their pastoral charm and slower-paced way of life. The largest and most densely populated is Saltspring, population 7,000; others on the main B.C. Ferry

Above — *On one side of Coal Harbor lie the office towers of Vancouver's financial district; on the other, the forested peninsula of Stanley Park with its grove of totems.* (B.C. Government)

Above — *Vancouver's Chinese heritage dates back to the time of the gold rush.* (Phil Hersee)

Above — *Apartment highrises line one side of Beach Avenue, English Bay beach the other. Left foreground — Aquatic Centre.* (Bill Staley)
Right — *School kids gather at the traditional Indian carving of a killer whale outside the aquarium in Stanley Park.* (Gunter Marx — Photo/Graphics)

The oldest part of Vancouver is known as Gastown, a name that commemorates "Gassy Jack" Deighton, one of the more colorful of the early inhabitants. The area has been restored, paved with old brick, its warehouses converted to boutiques. The flatiron building is a hotel.
(Phil Hersee)

route include North and South Pender, Galiano, Mayne and Gabriola, all with small resort, cottage and retirement communities.

Second city on Vancouver Island is Nanaimo, another former Hudson's Bay town and once the centre for productive coal mines. Today the forest and fishing industries sustain this city of 50,000 population. It has a direct link to the mainland via ferry from West Vancouver.

Port Alberni, population 20,000, the third largest community, is a forestry and mill town and a deep-sea port technically on the west coast, though it lies forty miles inland at the head of Alberni Inlet, nearer to the east coast than the west. The only road to cut across Vancouver Island, Highway 4, links Port Alberni to the east coast at Parksville, and to the west coast at Pacific Rim National Park and the two small fishing communities of Tofino and Ucluelet.

The *Lady Rose,* one of the last of the small, privately operated coastal ferries, still carries supplies and passengers from Port Alberni to such ports of call as Sarita and Bamfield, and through the beautiful Broken Islands in the mouth of Barkley Sound to Ucluelet. This handful of tiny islands is popular with canoeists. Transport of canoes is all part of the *Lady Rose* service. Pacific Rim Park, famous for its long, sandy beaches and wilderness forests, is becoming increasingly popular with tourists. Whale-watching cruises leave from Ucluelet during the migration months of summer.

The sheltered east coast of Vancouver Island is bordered by a narrow but fertile plain, one of the first areas of the province to be settled, logged and farmed. Here are located several one-industry towns founded mainly on the woods and milling industries, although with most of these the initial industry has declined and the towns now depend mainly

Top — *Vancouver's Chinatown publishes its own Chinese language newspaper, displayed daily in the windows. Even the city street names are in Chinese, as well as English.* (Ed Gifford — Photo/Graphics)
Left — *Four blocks of Pender Street constitute Chinatown's commercial heart, always busy with shoppers.* (Marin Petkov — Photo/Graphics)
Right — *For devotees of Oriental food, Chinatown is the place to go for fresh Chinese vegetables and other exotic ingredients.* (Vancouver Visitors Bureau)

Right — *Chinatown in winter: rain and boxes of mandarin oranges fresh off the boat.* (Jurgen Vogt — Photo/Graphics)

Top — *Wind surfers off West Vancouver.*
(Bill Staley)
Above — *Vancouver is a hotbed of English junior soccer.* (Phil Hersee)

Top — *Hang gliders soar above the North Shore mountains.* (Vancouver Visitors Bureau)
Above — *Cricket at Brockton Oval in Stanley Park — a die-hard English tradition.*
(B.C. Government)

Left — *Dawn at the mouth of the Capilano River and a lonely fisherman tries his luck. In the background, Lions Gate bridge.* (Bill Staley)

on tourism. Most have excellent beaches and provide good bases for sports fishing.

These towns, all with populations between four and five thousand, include Duncan, Crofton/Chemainus, Ladysmith and Parksville. The town of Chemainus, badly hit by mill closures, has recently found tourist fame by covering the walls of its buildings with painted murals of B.C. scenes.

Just north of Nanaimo are the towns of Courtenay, population nearly 9,000 and Comox, population nearly 7,000, site of a large Canadian Forces base. Farther north is Campbell River, population 16,000, about halfway up the island opposite Seymour Narrows and famous for boating (Desolation Sound on the mainland opposite is a popular destination) and sport fishing. In the tidal surges of the Narrows, fighting chinook salmon, known also as tyee or king, and cod provide irresistible enducements. Largest islands in the narrows are Quadra and Cortez, linked by ferry from Campbell River. At Cape Mudge on the southern tip of Quadra are many Indian petroglyphs and the Kwagiutl museum with its treasures of once confiscated potlatch materials.

Farther north along the east coast is Port McNeill, population three thousand, a small fishing and logging community with ferry connections to Cormorant and Malcolm islands. Alert Bay on Cormorant is a vital Kwagiutl community complete with totem poles (one the tallest in the world) and a cultural centre displaying tribal treasures. Malcolm Island was the locale of a Finnish attempt at a co-operative settlement around the turn of the century. Their centre, Sointula (Place of Harmony), is still home to blonde-haired descendants and the museum displays pioneer artifacts.

Port Hardy, population 6,000, at the northern end of the Vancouver Island highway, is summer jump-off point for B.C. Ferry service through the Inside Passage to Prince Rupert. Once a week the ferry calls in at the tiny fishing settlement of Bella Bella. (During the winter months, Prince Rupert service begins at Tsawwassen.) A fishing and logging community, Port Hardy is near the old HBC Fort Rupert, another turn-of-the-century coal-mining centre, and roads network south and southwest to tiny communities on

Left — *Frost-bite sailors in English Bay under the snowy peaks of Crown Mountain on Vancouver's North Shore.* (B.C. Government)

Right — *The Nanaimo-to-Vancouver annual bathtub race finishes with a flourish on Kitsilano Beach.* (Phil Hersee)

184

Quatsino Sound on the west coast, Coal Harbour, Holberg, Winter Harbour and Port Alice. The wilderness trail to Cape Scott Provincial Park begins near Holberg.

The mainland coast north of Vancouver is linked by ferries and roads as far as the fishing village of Lund, almost at the southern entrance to Desolation Sound. Communities along this Sunshine Coast, as it is called, include Gibson's Landing, Sechelt, Pender Harbour, Westview and Powell River. All but the latter, a pulp-mill town, are quiet havens for fishermen, boaters and tourists. Ferries connect Powell River with Comox on Vancouver Island, and Texada Island with its limestone quarries and iron-ore mine.

Above — *Bulk loading facilities at the new deep-sea port of Roberts Bank, built to handle coal from the southeast Rockies. The port is visible from the Tsawwassen ferry terminal.* (Bill Staley)
Left — *The port of Vancouver's chief shipment is lumber, product of B.C.'s vast forests.* (Greg Maurer — Photo/Graphics)

Above — *The new courthouse complex and open area at Robson Square features open-air restaurants in summer, ice-skating (under the dome) in winter.* (Phil Hersee)

Right — *The Museum of Anthropology at the University of B.C. stands on the Point Grey headland, its bold pillars reflecting the architecture of the Coast Indians. It and Robson Square Courthouse complex were designed by architect Arthur Erickson.* (Fred Chapman — Photo/Graphics)

Above — *The concrete posts and beams of the UBC Museum of Anthropology and large expanses of glass create exciting space inside for a world-famous collection of Northwest Indian artifacts.* (Vancouver Visitors Bureau)

Right — *On the top of Burnaby Mountain, Simon Fraser University, also designed by Arthur Erickson, is as well known for its architecture as for its educational facilities.* (Bill Staley)

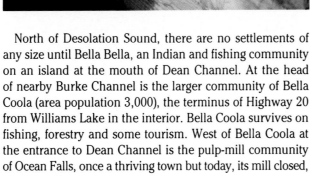

North of Desolation Sound, there are no settlements of any size until Bella Bella, an Indian and fishing community on an island at the mouth of Dean Channel. At the head of nearby Burke Channel is the larger community of Bella Coola (area population 3,000), the terminus of Highway 20 from Williams Lake in the interior. Bella Coola survives on fishing, forestry and some tourism. West of Bella Coola at the entrance to Dean Channel is the pulp-mill community of Ocean Falls, once a thriving town but today, its mill closed, almost a ghost town.

Settlement on the far north coast is sparse. Only a few small logging camps and Indian settlements are sprinkled along a shoreline that is steep and intricately indented. At the head of Douglas Channel, however, some seventy-five miles from the open ocean, is Kitimat, a port city of 13,500, founded around an aluminim smelter in the 1950s and now also the site of a large pulp and paper mill. It was the availability of cheap hydro-electric power in the area, not raw materials, that caused the smelter to be located here — the bauxite ore is shipped in mainly from Jamaica.

Kitimat is linked by road to Highway 16, the Yellowhead Highway linking Prince Rupert on the coast with Prince George, Jasper and Edmonton, Alberta. Next to Greater Vancouver, Prince Rupert, population 17,000, is the largest city on the B.C. mainland coast. Like Vancouver, Prince Rupert was founded as the terminus of a continental railway. The Grand Trunk Pacific (later the Canadian National) built from Edmonton to Fort George in 1908, then forged west down the Skeena to the Pacific, where it supposed a new world port would spring up. While the new railway spurred settlement and logging all along the Skeena River, Prince Rupert never lived up to expectation, even though it is nearer

Opposite and top left — *English customs persist in the rural Fraser Valley. The huntsmen ride in red coats with their hounds — but the bloodsport has been tamed. The dogs chase merely a scent, not a live fox.* (Both by Phil Hersee)

Above — *The spires of St. Paul's Church, North Vancouver, mimic the twin peaks of The Lions, above.* (Phil Hersee)

Left — *In summer, the steam train Royal Hudson makes the trip from North Vancouver to Squamish along scenic Howe Sound.* (B.C. Government)

Above — *Ridley Island near Prince Rupert, site of a new bulk-handling deep-sea terminal for coal from the northeast fields.* (B.C. Government)
Top right — *Industry grew up along the Fraser River — and remains there still. Barges transport wood chips to the processing plants.* (B.C. Government)
Right — *Fishing nets at Alert Bay, village on Cormorant Inland at the north end of Vancouver Island.* (Marin Petkov — Photo/Graphics)

Above — *B.C. Department of Transport ferry "Kwuna" links Alliford Bay on Moresby Island and Skidegate on Graham Island in the Queen Charlottes. Sailing time is 20 minutes.* (Jurgen Vogt — Photo/Graphics)
Left — *Port Hardy is a fishing community on the north coast of Vancouver Island and terminus for the B.C. ferry Inside Passage service to Prince Rupert.* (Gunter Marx — Photo/Graphics)

193

to prairie grain and to markets in Asia than is Vancouver. For most of this century it has depended upon fishing and fish processing for its livelihood. It is today headquarters of the northern fishing fleet.

Lately, however, with the development of B.C.'s northeast coalfields, the opening of a new bulk shipping terminus at nearby Ridley Island, and pulp- and paper-mill construction, Prince Rupert's economy has flourished. It's the northern terminus of the B.C. Ferry system, the southern terminus of the Alaska system. In addition, ferry service is maintained between the city and Skidegate, a settlement on the Queen Charlotte Islands. Sports fishing, both fresh and saltwater, and big-game hunting are popular.

Most northerly of the B.C. coast communities is Stewart, population 2,000, at the end of long and skinny Portland Canal, the boundary with Alaska, its fortunes ebbing and flowing with the fate of the huge Granduc iron mine. Stewart has highway connections north to Cassiar and the Alaska Highway, south via the Nass River to Highway 16.

The Queen Charlotte Islands, an archipelago of two large islands and about 150 small ones, lie some sixty miles

The ornate legislative buildings at one end of Victoria harbor are backed by the distant peaks of the Olympic Mountains, Washington. (B.C. Government)

Above — *Red double-decker buses are a Victoria trademark, along with the earliest spring blooms in Canada.* (B.C. Government)

Right — *Totems in Victoria's Thunderbird Park provide a striking foreground for the turn-of-the-century Empress Hotel.* (B.C. Government)

Far right — *Legislative buildings, Victoria, framed in English roses.* (B.C. Government)

Sailboats, canoes, planes — the B.C. Coast provides endless
recreational opportunities. This is Princess Margaret Marine Park, one
of several designed for eater-access only. (Lyn Hancock)

offshore, the most far-flung of all Canada's islands and one of the least populated regions of the B.C. Coast. Of the total population of around 6,000, nearly all is concentrated in the northeast. Masset on the north coast is the largest centre, with a population of around 2,000; another 3,000 are clustered around Skidegate Inlet in Queen Charlotte City, Sandspit, Port Clements and Skidegate. The only public roads are those linking these settlements: the rest of the islands are generally inaccessible except by boat or plane.

Most residents of the Queen Charlottes are employed in fishing or the woods industry, though tourism, particularly special-interest group tours, is increasing. The islands are a haven for wildlife and contain priceless relics of Indian culture. Much of the population of the islands is Haida Indian, a tribe which has kept a strong cultural identity and is particularly well known for its art traditions. The Haida, whose ancestral village sites are found all over the islands, have recently launched extensive land title claims against the B.C. government (no treaties with these Indians were ever signed). The Haida say that all the Queen Charlotte Islands belong to them, and in 1985 they were actively trying to stop logging on Lyell Island off South Moresby, part of an area proposed as a new national park. The islands' rich reserves of spruce and cedar are among the last unlogged virgin forests along the B.C. Coast. Ecologists and the Indians want preservation, not development.

Centennial Square in downtown Victoria is graced by a fountain and a traditional English Knot garden. (B.C. Government)

Alaska Geographic® Back Issues

One Man's Wilderness, Vol. 1, No. 2. The story of a dream shared by many, fulfilled by a few; a man goes into the Bush, builds a cabin and shares his incredible wilderness experience. Color photos. 116 pages, $9.95.

Admiralty . . . Island in Contention, Vol. 1, No. 3. An intimate and multifaceted view of Admiralty; it's geological and historical past, its present-day geography, wildlife and sparse human population. Color photos. 78 pages, $5.

Fisheries of the North Pacific: History, Species, Gear & Processes, Vol. 1, No. 4. Out of print. (Book edition available)

The Alaska-Yukon Wild Flowers Guide, Vol. 2, No. 1. Out of print. (Book edition available)

Glacier Bay: Old Ice, New Land, Vol. 3, No. 1. The expansive wilderness of southeastern Alaska's Glacier Bay National Monument (recently proclaimed a national park and preserve) unfolds in crisp text and color photographs. Records the flora and fauna of the area, its natural history, with hike and cruise information, plus a large-scale color map. 132 pages, $11.95.

Richard Harrington's Antarctic, Vol. 3, No. 3. The Canadian photojournalist guides readers through remote and little understood regions of the Antarctic and subantarctic. More than 200 color photos and a large fold-out map. 104 pages, $8.95.

Southeast: Alaska's Panhandle, Vol. 5, No. 2. Explores southeastern Alaska's maze of fjords and islands, mossy forests and glacier-draped mountains — from Dixon Entrance to Icy Bay, including all of the state's fabled Inside Passage. Along the way are profiles of every town, together with a look at the region's history, economy, people, attractions and future. Includes large fold-out map and seven area maps. 192 pages, $12.95.

Alaska Whales and Whaling, Vol. 5, No. 4. The wonders of whales in Alaska — their life cycles, travels and travails — are examined, with an authoritative history of commercial and subsistence whaling in the North. Includes a fold-out poster of 14 major whale species in Alaska in perspective, color photos and illustrations, with historical photos and line drawings. 144 pages, $12.95.

The Aurora Borealis, Vol. 6, No. 2. The northern lights — in ancient times seen as a dreadful forecast of doom, in modern days an inspiration to countless poets. What causes the aurora, how it works, how and why scientists are studying it today and its implications for our future. 96 pages, $7.95.

Alaska's Native People, Vol. 6, No. 3. Examine the varied worlds of the Inupiat Eskimo, Yup'ik Eskimo, Athabascan, Aleut, Tlingit, Haida and Tsimshian. Included are sensitive, informative articles by Native writers, plus a large, four-color map detailing the Native villages and defining the language areas, 304 pages, $24.95.

The Stikine, Vol. 6, No. 4. River route to three Canadian gold strikes in the 1800s, the Stikine is the largest and most navigable of several rivers that flow from northwestern Canada through southeastern Alaska on their way to the sea. Illustrated with contemporary color photos and historic black-and-white; includes a large fold-out map. 96 pages, $9.95.

Alaska's Great Interior, Vol. 7, No. 1. Alaska's rich Interior country, west from the Alaska-Yukon Territory border and including the huge drainage between the Alaska Range and the Brooks Range, is covered thoroughly. Included are the region's people, communities, history, economy, wilderness areas and wildlife. Illustrated with contemporary color and black-and-white photos. Includes a large fold-out map. 128 pages, $9.95.

A Photographic Geography of Alaska, Vol. 7, No. 2. An overview of the entire state — a visual tour through the six regions of Alaska: Southeast, Southcentral/Gulf Coast, Alaska Peninsula and Aleutians, Bering Sea Coast, Arctic and Interior. Plus a handy appendix of valuable information — "Facts About Alaska." Revised in 1983. Approximately 160 color and black-and-white photos and 35 maps. 192 pages, $15.95.

The Aleutians, Vol. 7, No. 3. Home of the Aleut, a tremendous wildlife spectacle, a major World War II battleground and now the heart of a thriving new commercial fishing industry. Contemporary color and black-and-white photographs, and a large fold-out map. 224 pages, $14.95.

Klondike Lost: A Decade of Photographs by Kinsey & Kinsey, Vol. 7, No. 4. An album of rare photographs and all-new text about the lost Klondike boom town of Grand Forks, second in size only to Dawson during the gold rush. $12.95.

Wrangell-Saint Elias, Vol. 8, No. 1. Mountains, including the continent's second- and fourth-highest peaks, dominate this international wilderness that sweeps from the Wrangell Mountains in Alaska to the southern Saint Elias range in Canada. Includes a large fold-out map. 144 pages, $9.95.

Alaska Mammals, Vol. 8, No. 2. From tiny ground squirrels to the powerful polar bear, and from the tundra to the magnificent whales inhabiting Alaska's waters, this volume includes 80 species of mammals found in Alaska. 184 pages, $12.95.

The Kotzebue Basin, Vol. 8, No. 3. Examines northwestern Alaska's thriving trading area of Kotzebue Sound and the Kobuk and Noatak river basins, lifelines of the region's Inupiat Eskimos, early explorers, and present-day, hardy residents. 184 pages, $12.95.

Alaska National Interest Lands, Vol. 8, No. 4. Following passage of the bill formalizing Alaska's national interest land selections (d-2 lands), longtime Alaskans Celia Hunter and Ginny Wood review each selection, outlining location, size, access, and briefly describing the region's special attractions. 242 pages, $14.95.

Alaska's Glaciers, Vol. 9, No. 1. Examines in depth the massive rivers of ice, their composition, exploration, present-day distribution and scientific significance. 144 pages, $10.95.

Sitka and Its Ocean/Island World, Vol. 9, No. 2. From the elegant capital of Russian America to a beautiful but modern port, Sitka, on Baranof Island, has become a commercial and cultural center for southeastern Alaska. 128 pages, $9.95.

Islands of the Seals: The Pribilofs, Vol. 9, No. 3. Great herds of northern fur seals drew Russians and Aleuts to these remote Bering Sea islands where they founded permanent communities and established a unique international commerce. 128 pages, $9.95.

Alaska's Oil/Gas & Minerals Industry, Vol. 9, No. 4. Experts detail the geological processes and resulting mineral and fossil fuel resources that are now in the forefront of Alaska's economy. Illustrated with historical black-and-white and contemporary color photographs. 216 pages, $12.95.

Adventure Roads North: The Story of the Alaska Highway and Other Roads in _The MILEPOST_®, Vol. 10, No. 1. From Alaska's first highway — the Richardson — to the famous Alaska Highway, first overland route to the 49th state, text and photos provide a history of Alaska's roads and take a mile-by-mile look at the country they cross. 224 pages, $14.95.

ANCHORAGE and the Cook Inlet Basin, Vol. 10, No. 2. "Anchorage country" . . . the Kenai, the Susitna Valley, and Matanuska. Heavily illustrated in color and including three illustrated maps . . . one an uproarious artist's forecast of "Anchorage 2035." 168 pages, $14.95.

Alaska's Salmon Fisheries, Vol. 10, No. 3. The work of _ALASKA_® magazine Outdoors Editor Jim Rearden, this issue takes a comprehensive look at Alaska's most valuable commercial fishery. 128 pages, $12.95.

Up the Koyukuk, Vol. 10, No. 4. Highlights the Koyukuk region of north-central Alaska . . . the wildlife, fauna, Native culture and more. 152 pages. $14.95.

Nome: City of the Golden Beaches, Vol. 11, No. 1. The colorful history of Alaska's most famous gold rush town has never been told like this before. Illustrated with hundreds of rare black-and-white photos, the book traces the story of Nome from the crazy days of the 1900 gold rush. 184 pages, $14.95.

Alaska's Farms and Gardens, Vol. 11, No. 2. An overview of the past, present, and future of agriculture in Alaska, and a wealth of information on how to grow your own fruit and vegetables in the north. 144 pages, $12.95.

Chilkat River Valley, Vol. 11, No. 3. This issue explores the mountain-rimmed valley at the head of the Inside Passage, its natural resources, and those hardy residents who make their home along the Chilkat. 112 pages, $12.95.

Alaska Steam, Vol. 11, No. 4. A pictorial history of the Alaska Steamship Company pioneering the northern travel lanes. Compiled by Lucile McDonald. More than 100 black-and-white historical photos. 160 pages. $12.95.

Northwest Territories, Vol. 12, No. 1. An in-depth look at some of the most beautiful and isolated land in North America. Compiled by Richard Harrington. 148 color photos. 136 pages. $12.95.

Alaska's Forest Resources, Vol. 12, No. 2 examines the majestic and valuable forests of Alaska. Nearly 200 historical black-and-white and color photos. 200 pages. $14.95.

Alaska Native Arts and Crafts, Vol. 12, No. 3. An in-depth look at the art and artifacts of Alaska's Native people. More than 200 full color photos. 215 pages. $17.95.

Our Arctic Year, Vol. 12, No. 4. Vivian and Gil Staender's simple, compelling story of a year in the wilds of the Brooks Range of Alaska, with only birds, nature and an unspoiled land. They share their discoveries, and their reactions to a year of isolation with time to sense their surroundings. Over 100 color photos. 150 pages. $12.95.

Where Mountains Meet the Sea: Alaska's Gulf Coast, Vol. 13, No. 1. Alaskan's first-hand descriptions of the 850-mile arc that crowns the Pacific Ocean from Kodiak and surrounding islands to Cape Yakataga. Included is a historical overview of this area, and a close look at the geological forces that constantly reshape its landscape. More than 300 photos. 191 pages. $14.95.

British Columbia Coast/The Canadian Inside Passage, Vol. 13, No. 3. Where to go, how to get there, what you'll find on the B.C. Coast west of the Coast Mountain divide, including Vancouver Island and the Queen Charlottes. Brief historical background (indigenous residents, fur trade, exploration, European settlers) and current conditions. Includes large fold-out map. $14.95.

FORTHCOMING ISSUE:
Lake Clark/Iliamna, Vol. 13, No. 4. This issue explores the natural and human history of not only Lake Clark and Iliamna Lake, but also the surrounding countryside. This region is considered to be the epitome of Alaska's geography.

ALL PRICES SUBJECT TO CHANGE.

Your $30 membership in the Alaska Geographic Society includes 4 subsequent issues of _ALASKA GEOGRAPHIC®_, the Society's official quarterly. Please add $4 for non-U.S. membership.

Additional membership information available upon request. Single copies of the _ALASKA GEOGRAPHIC®_ back issues are also available. When ordering, please make payments in U.S. funds and add $1 postage/handling per copy. To order back issues send your check or money order and volumes desired to:

The Alaska Geographic Society

P.O. Box 93370, Anchorage, Alaska 99509